W9-CZJ-386

FATAL
MISTAKES

ALSO BY KEVIN MARRON

Ritual Abuse
Witches, Pagans and Magic in the New Age
Apprenticed in Crime

FATAL MISTAKES

The Disturbing Events That Led to
the Murder of Nina de Villiers and a
Nationwide Campaign Against Violence

▼

Kevin Marron

Doubleday Canada Limited

Copyright © Kevin Marron 1993
All rights reserved. No part of this publication may be reproduced, stored in a
retrieval system, or transmitted, in any form or by any means, electronic,
mechanical, photocopying, recording or otherwise, without the prior written
permission of Doubleday Canada Limited.

Canadian Cataloguing in Publishing Data

Marron, Kevin

    Fatal mistakes: the disturbing events that led
to the murder of Nina de Villiers and a nationwide
campaign against violence

ISBN 0-385-25439-3

1. Yeo, Jonathan. 2. De Villiers, Nina, d. 1991.
3. Murder - Ontario - Hamilton. 4. Violence (Law) -
Canada. 5. CAVEAT (Organization). I. Title

HV6535.C33H35 1993   364.1'523'092   C93-094423-2

Photo of Nina de Villiers by Essence School Photography
Photo of Jonathon Yeo by Canapress Photo Service
Jacket design by William Laughton
Printed and bound in the USA

"Give us Back the Night," Cynthia Kerr,
Strings Attached Publishing: SOCAN, 1989.
Used by permission. All rights reserved.

Published in Canada by
Doubleday Canada Limited
105 Bond Street
Toronto, Ontario
M5B 1Y3

To the memory of
Nina de Villiers and all victims
of violent crime.

Contents

▼

Acknowledgements

▼

I WOULD LIKE TO THANK Priscilla de Villiers for helping with this book in many different ways. She provided me with a detailed and insightful account of her own background, Nina's life and the circumstances of her death. She also put me in touch with Nina's teachers and friends. Priscilla and other members of CAVEAT informed me of the issues involved in their campaign against violence. Although it was very difficult for her to deal with the material presented in this book, Priscilla reviewed portions of my manuscript, making many helpful suggestions and correcting factual errors.

I would also like to thank Etienne de Villiers for his perceptive comments about Nina. Among the CAVEAT members who have provided me with invaluable information were Dorothy Leonard, Ann Walsh, Carole Walzak, Pam Suzuki, Judy Gordon, Morag Smith and Yvonne Cox. Many of Nina's friends were also most helpful, especially Sheila Singh, Simon Blackstone, Chris Forrest, Karen Deme and Stefen Powell. Cathy Crowder and Cynthia Kerr each provided further insight, as did Nina's tennis coach Sam Rifaat and the teachers at Hillfield-Strathallan College: John Beaver, Richard Cunningham, Blanka Guyatt, Mark Hudson, John McGuirk, Jay Parry and Michaele Robertson.

I am most grateful to James and Laura Yeo for sharing their

understanding of James's brother, Jonathan. Many of the people involved in the inquest into Jonathan's death were most helpful. I would particularly like to thank Ontario Chief Coroner James Young, his staff and the Ontario Provincial Police officers assisting him, together with lawyers Ted Minden, Mark Sandler and Ray Harris. Other journalists covering the inquest helped me in different ways, particularly Jill Morison and Norman de Bono of the *Hamilton Spectator* and Paul Kidd of the *Toronto Star*.

My friend Susan Goodman spent many hours discussing the book with me and reading early drafts. I am always grateful for her insight and astute advice. I would also like to thank Joanna Chapman for her helpful suggestions.

My agent, Dean Cooke, provided me with input at the earliest stages of this project and has been highly supportive ever since. Sarah Silberstein Swartz edited the manuscript with her usual sensitivity and expertise. People at Doubleday Canada Limited have shown the utmost professionalism in their handling of this book. I would particularly like to thank editor-in-chief John Pearce, production editor Christine Harrison and publicity director Dara Rowland.

Prologue
GIVE US BACK
THE NIGHT

▼

L IKE MANY WOMEN across Canada, Nina de Villiers was intensely disturbed by the "Montreal massacre." An 18-year-old high
school student with an interest in science, she could easily identify
with the 14 female engineering students who were killed when a
lone gunman invaded their class at the University of Montreal's
l'Ecole Polytechnique on December 6, 1989.

It was a crime that had a profound impact on Canadians,
sounding an alarm about escalating violence against women, while
prompting people to confront this issue in their own communities
and in their personal lives. For several months, it remained the subject of ardent debate in the media and in private conversations.

Nina discussed the issue many times with her mother, Priscilla.
In one conversation in the living room of their suburban home in
Burlington, Ontario, Nina rhetorically asked, "Do you realize that
it could have been me or one of my friends who was shot?"

Priscilla would have reason to remember this conversation for
the rest of her life.

It was January 1990 and they were talking about whether Nina
should participate in a music video to honour the 14 students who
had been killed. Nina was in her last year of high school. A well-
trained singer and member of several choirs, she had agreed to sing
background vocals in a recording which would promote awareness

about violence against women and raise money for a scholarship fund for female engineering students.

Nina had just learned that the 14-hour recording session was scheduled on the eve of important high school exams. Her mother had questioned whether it was wise for Nina to take part, especially as it would also mean a 60-kilometre drive to a Toronto recording studio. But a stubborn refusal to let anyone interfere with her own agenda was one of the few faults that Priscilla was prepared to recognize in Nina, who put an end to all further discussion of the issue by telling her mother, "Look, I feel really strongly about this and I'm going to do it."

Nina had been overwhelmed by the horror of the crime committed by a man dressed in battle fatigues who burst into a classroom armed with an automatic rifle, separated the men from the women and proceeded to execute as many women as he could, before taking his own life. It was at the same time a random and a deliberate act. It did not matter to Marc Lepine who his victims were, providing they were women occupying a place in society that he thought should belong to men.

Violence against women was too often ignored or made light of, but here was a crime of such magnitude that society had to take notice. The song that Nina helped record spoke for the women who were killed in Montreal and a multitude of others whose deaths and suffering had attracted little public attention:

> *Too many spirits have been broken*
> *Too many dreams have been crushed*
> *Too many stood in the darkness*
> *Listening to the hush.*

At the recording session on January 20, 1990, the video camera panned along the line of background vocalists as they sang:

Who's going to break this silence
Who's going to fight the fight
Stand up and be counted
And give us back the night.

Nina seemed oblivious to the camera which lingered on her for a few moments. She was a study in energy and concentration. Her lively face was framed by a set of headphones. Her blonde curly hair, cut short at one side, sprang out on the other from over the headphone in a wild, eccentric shock. She was listening intently, bobbing her head as she focused on the score that fluttered in her hands in front of her. Her lips quivered with conviction as she sang, "Give women back the night."

Just nineteen months later, the video footage would be used in an altogether different context after Nina was abducted on the evening of August 9, 1991. The images of Nina, alert, creative and fired with idealism, would be cut up and frozen to be shown in television news clips and public service messages. They would be used in a desperate search for yet another woman who had been taken from the night.

The quiet, prosperous community where Nina grew up had been shaken earlier that summer. In June, the body of another teenager, Leslie Mahaffy of Burlington, was found encased in concrete in a reservoir. Meanwhile local residents were following the disturbing testimony that emerged at the murder trial of a 53-year-old drifter who stumbled upon a young woman sunbathing on a secluded section of Burlington's Lake Ontario shoreline and stabbed her eight times, subsequently boasting to a cell mate that he had "ripped her apart." Eight months after Nina's murder, the body of 15-year-old Kristen French, abducted from near her home in St. Catharines, was found in a ditch beside a country road on the outskirts of Burlington.

The daily toll of violent crime leaves many people at a loss as to how to direct their outrage or focus their concern. While victims' families and friends are still struggling with their suffering and grief, the media present the public with fresh crimes to contemplate. New names are added to the litany of victims, soon to be forgotten and replaced with others. Like viewers of a horror movie, people are continually shocked but ultimately numbed by the accumulation of violence which they see, hear or read about. They feel profoundly disturbed, but impotent, as they silently change the channel or turn the page.

I, too, turned the page when I first read about Nina's murder. In fact, I wrote one of the brief stories in the *Globe and Mail* which recorded the steps in the investigation of her death and then moved on to concern myself with other events and different issues. But the story of Nina's death kept returning to the headlines as facts emerged about her killer, Jonathan Yeo, who shot himself in a police chase soon after the murders of Nina and his other victim, a 28-year-old New Brunswick woman, Karen Marquis.

The life and death of Jonathan Yeo, and the circumstances surrounding his crimes, were probed at a 44-day coroner's inquest in the summer of 1992. The extensive evidence showed that he had been assaulting and abusing women for years, but had slipped through cracks in every system designed to protect the public from violent crime. As I sat through each day of that inquest, I was shocked by the extent of the bungling and carelessness that were exposed. Society's failure to deal with sexual predators and violence against women was illustrated more clearly in this case than in any other that I have ever encountered in 15 years as a journalist.

Evidence at the inquest provided the source material for Jonathan's story, which is told in Part Two of this book. Reporters at the inquest were asked to conceal the identity of some of the witnesses, female victims of Jonathan's predatory violence. I have respected this request and have given pseudonyms to these women.

With the exception of these pseudonyms, which are clearly identified as such, everyone quoted or referred to in the book is identified by his or her real name.

This book is not only about a killer who fell through the cracks and the system that failed to stop him. It is primarily the story of his victim, a woman who never met Jonathan Yeo until her last terrifying moments, yet whose life depended on someone comprehending and dealing with Yeo's problems or keeping them at bay. Because nobody did that, it was up to those who loved Nina to make sure that lessons were learned from her death in order that other potential victims might be better protected.

This book begins and ends with the story of Nina de Villiers. It begins with an account of a rich and promising life that was cut short by a random act of violence. It is usually only the names of killers who live on in popular memory and not those of their victims. For example, many people in Canada remember Marc Lepine as the perpetrator of the Montreal massacre, but few could name any of the 14 women who died. It is partly to redress this balance, to give due weight to a victim's life, that I am telling Nina's story, which I have learned from her family, teachers and friends.

As I found out more about her life, I came to understand the different ways in which those close to her were affected by their loss. I could see how her personality and her values inspired and gave form to the grass-roots campaign against violent crime that emerged following her death. This campaign, which I describe near the end of the book, is linked to the story of Nina, whose memory it helps keep alive.

While this book is the story of an individual victim and all the circumstances that surround her death, it is also a study of how a community responds emotionally, socially and politically to violent crime. What can we do to help victims and their families? What can we do to protect other potential victims? How can we deal with a homicidal sexual predator in our midst? These are among the questions that I have set out to investigate in this book — along with one very basic question that was posed by one of Nina's closest school friends, "How can a society that produced someone as beautiful as Nina also produce something as ugly as the crime that killed her?"

I knew that I wanted to write this book almost as soon as I met Priscilla de Villiers about six months after her daughter's death. She immediately impressed me as a force to be reckoned with, an intellectually sharp woman whose voice, with its refined South African accent, spoke with precision and an air of authority. I was drawn by her apparent moral integrity, as well as the emotional depth and resonance of the story she had to tell.

She was a participant in a public forum on the justice system at which a senior member of the National Parole Board had been invited to speak. I was assigned to cover the meeting for the *Globe and Mail*, since there was the prospect of fiery confrontation over the early release of violent offenders. In fact, there was no confrontation as the parole board representative got stuck in a snow storm and failed to appear. But a large crowd had gathered in the Hamilton Convention Centre, and it was seething with emotions. People lined up in front of microphones to speak about relatives and friends who had been murdered and to rail against a justice system that failed to protect their loved ones' lives.

Though one had to be moved by the personal statements on the impact of violent crime, I felt uncomfortable about the implications that were being drawn from their harrowing testimonies. I was uneasy about the vehemence of the many calls for draconian punishments and the enthusiastic applause these evoked. When a prominent Hamilton lawyer, a former Crown attorney, spoke in defence of the age-old principle of the presumption of innocence until proven guilty, he was jeered and shouted down by the audience.

I was therefore apprehensive about what message we would hear from Priscilla de Villiers when she rose to field an emotionally charged question about bringing back the death penalty. I was amazed at the moderation of her response, delivered in a controlled voice that nevertheless rang with passion and obvious pain. She explained that it was an abhorrence of violence that had brought her to Canada from her native South Africa. She said she did not believe in capital punishment and was not seeking vengeance. After a meticulously reasoned account of the failings of the justice system in relation to her daughter's death, she expressed her fear that a loss of confidence in our democratic laws and institutions could lead to vigilante justice and the kind of anarchic violence that plagued her homeland.

What she had to say about the danger of people taking the law into their own hands made sense to me in view of the rage that had erupted in the audience that night. My sympathy and curiosity were aroused by the portrait which Priscilla had painted of herself as a woman with a life-long commitment to social justice and democratic institutions who had been forced to reassess her beliefs. Her daughter had been murdered by a man who was free on bail while awaiting trial for a violent sexual offence. Nina de Villiers had perhaps been betrayed by the concept of civil liberties that her mother had always cherished.

After the forum, I met Priscilla and members of the citizens' group that she was spearheading in a campaign to reform the justice system. I was intrigued by the combination of passionate commitment and quirkiness that I found. This group had started around a coffee table and expanded into a nation-wide campaign. Most of the members were women who tended to undervalue their skills and previous work experience as homemakers and volunteers for community charities. Yet they had built an efficient and influential organization and had already garnered hundreds of thousands of names on a petition calling for legislative change. The group bore the erudite but very apt name CAVEAT, which means "a warning" and is a legal term for an order that certain parties be given a hearing before any action is taken on a particular matter. It is an acronym for "Canadians Against Violence Everywhere Advocating its Termination."

The group was founded by women who belonged to the tennis club around which Nina was jogging when she was abducted. They all lived in what had seemed like a very protected, affluent suburban community. The spate of unrelated violent crimes that had beset Burlington in recent months seemed like an anathema to residents who tended to look upon their city as a haven from the social ills that infected less privileged parts of the world. Priscilla herself was an artist, the wife of a neurosurgeon, who had enjoyed the peace and seclusion of her home on the shore of Burlington Bay, painting vibrantly coloured landscapes and enjoying a close relationship with her family.

The violent intrusion that transformed Priscilla's life also galvanized her friends, neighbours and acquaintances, who suddenly realized that their community was not well protected. They and their children — particularly their daughters — could no longer feel safe on the quiet tree-lined streets near their homes. They were horror-struck by the thought that an armed psychopath in search of human prey had found a perfect hunting ground around the large lots and abundant park land that had made Burlington such a desirable place to live.

Thousands of distraught residents volunteered to help search for Nina and overwhelmed the de Villiers family with constant outpourings of sympathy and condolence. After the discovery of Nina's body, the energy that inspired the search was channelled by family and friends into a public campaign that would ensure that Nina would not be another forgotten victim.

As Priscilla worked indefatigably for CAVEAT, she anguished about constantly exposing her family's private grief to public scrutiny. She worried that she might be trading on her daughter's memory by using her murder as a marketing tool to promote her campaign. But, she told me, her husband, Rocco, reminded her that it was what Nina would have done. In fact, their daughter had told them her views on a very similar issue while she was working on the video about the Montreal massacre.

When the video was shown on the "Much Music" cable television channel, Nina and her friends had been excited and proud of their achievement, but at the same time conscious of the horrible reality that had inspired their work. Nina discussed her anxiety over this conflict with her family and with Cynthia Kerr, who wrote the video's song. Having a video aired on "Much Music" is a hallmark of success for musicians in Canada. Kerr and Chantal Chamerland, her partner in the folk duo Open Mind, shared Nina's concern that people might question their motives, even though they were dedicating all the proceeds from the recording to a scholarship fund for female engineering students.

This was an issue they earnestly debated in many conversations, but they always came to the same conclusions. They felt compelled to do something to raise awareness about the terrible event and about the ongoing threat to public safety. There was no point in feeling guilty about the natural pride that one takes in doing a good job or the pleasure and excitement one derives from working with others in a common cause.

Priscilla often took strength from her memory of Nina's involvement in the Montreal massacre video. But it was, of course, a memory that resonated with bitter irony. The song that Nina helped to record was a lament for the shattered dreams of the 14 women who died and of all women who no longer feel secure in their communities. The lyrics of one of the verses were:

> *Can't go to the city park*
> *Can't go on the bus*
> *Can't go walking after dark*
> *'Cause God knows what will happen to us.*

What made this irony even more acute was that Nina had

always been conscious of the need for personal safety. She seldom went out at night unaccompanied. On the night of a party that followed the release of the video, Nina asked a friend to walk her to her car, which she had cautiously parked under a street light. Cynthia Kerr noticed this and remarked that Nina seemed to have paid attention to the message of the song, one of the lines of which referred to women taking such precautions. Nina replied that she always did.

Nina had been particularly nervous about the security arrangements for the recording session and had spent hours discussing them on the phone. Part of the video was to be shot outside the studio and Nina was afraid that someone might see the video as an act of provocation and respond violently. After all, Lepine had been provoked by the mere fact that women were gaining entry to a traditionally male field of employment.

Like many Canadian women in the aftermath of the Montreal massacre, Nina had begun to worry about her own safety in situations where she would previously not have given it a second thought. Many women saw Lepine's actions as an extreme expression of a pattern of male violence and sexism which is endemic in society. The massacre became a focus for anger and grief over the daily toll of domestic violence, sexual assault and harassment in women's lives. It sometimes seemed that all men were being held responsible for Lepine's actions. Some men responded to this with a rage and hostility that seemed to confirm many feminists' analysis. Sick jokes by male students and slogans scrawled on college walls created a climate which heightened women's fears that they could no longer feel safe on the streets, at work or in classrooms.

The Montreal massacre had sent out a clear message that no woman was safe. Nothing short of security check points and metal detectors at classroom doors could have saved those young women once Lepine had formulated his plan and armed himself with an automatic rifle. The women sitting in their classroom at the engi-

neering school had no conceivable reason to believe that they needed to protect themselves from a possible attack. What they were
doing was not even remotely political or provocative in anyone's
mind but that of Marc Lepine. The struggles for women to gain
access to institutions like engineering schools were fought by previous generations. The presence of women at l'Ecole Polytechnique
was taken for granted by almost everyone at the school, males and
females alike. The students who were killed did not even think of
themselves as feminists. One of the students said as much to Lepine
before he shot her.

What might have protected those young women were some
measures to ensure that Lepine never had access to such deadly
weaponry. People were alarmed by the notion that there may be
other Marc Lepines at large in the community with easy access to
all the fire power they needed to fulfil their demented fantasies.
That is why parents of those victims campaigned for better gun
control laws. Some changes did come, but they were too little and
too late for Nina, whose mother grimly joined the gun control lobbying campaign.

In the months that followed the Montreal massacre, it seemed
as though it was beginning to dawn on the Canadian public that
violent crime had reached a level that could no longer be tolerated.
There was a growing consensus that something must be done to
allow ordinary people to safely pursue their everyday lives.

Yet two years later, in December 1991, little had changed
except that there were more victims to remember. Nina's earnest
discussions about women's autonomy were almost too painful to
recall, yet unforgettable for Priscilla, as she attended the memorial
to the victims of the Montreal massacre. Numbly she stood with
the families of other victims, silently holding a candle for those 14
young women who wanted to be engineers, for countless other
women whose lives have been cut short by violence and for Nina,
who wanted the world to learn something from the tragic loss.

Part One
NINA

one

VIOLENCE IN
SOUTH AFRICA

▼

NINA WAS A GENTLE, loving and gifted young woman with a wide range of interests and burgeoning skills. But my purpose in telling her story is not to suggest that she was an exceptional person or that her life counted for more than any other. Rather, it is to make sure that we give due value to the life of anyone who is needlessly killed. Nor do I intend to sanctify or sentimentalize Nina. Any attempt to do so would fail to do justice to her memory and would tend to simplify or trivialize the issues that flow from her death.

If I present few glaring faults in her character, that is simply because I did not find many, even though I was satisfied that I had obtained a fairly complete picture from many different sources. Perhaps, if Nina had been allowed to live, she may have quarrelled with her parents, rebelled or grown away from them. She may have experimented with different lifestyles or adopted other values. People would have been surprised if she had done any of those things since she had enjoyed harmonious relationships with her family and her peers throughout her teenage years. She had seemed to be remarkably comfortable with herself and her place in the world. But it is impossible to say what she would have done; she was deprived of having her adult life unfold. Now her life story must inevitably be linked with that of those who loved her, particularly that of her mother, Priscilla, whose campaign keeps Nina's memory alive.

When I interviewed Priscilla for this book, we met in the coffee shop at the tennis club near which her daughter was last seen alive. We planned to conduct the interview in her office, but Priscilla had forgotten her keys and suggested the tennis club because it was close by. At first it seemed to me a brave act of defiance to choose this of all locations. But then I realized that almost everywhere Priscilla went held painful memories and there was no way that she could ever escape her loss. She was, in fact, determined to confront her loss and communicate its full impact.

At first, Priscilla impressed me as being very tough and self-assured. But as we talked, she revealed herself as a sensitive, thoughtful person who continually questioned herself and her motives and worried about other people's feelings and responses. In spite of the grim subjects we were discussing, I was often entertained by her irrepressible wit and an intellect that she cannot stop from taking tangents. Occasionally she was overwhelmed with sorrow, but for most of the time she won her private battle to keep her emotions under control, as she focused on telling me the story of her daughter's life.

It would be hard to tell Nina's story without telling that of her parents. The values they transmitted to Nina and the stories they told were central in her life. Nina was six years old when the family left South Africa and would not have remembered much about her life there. But she and her brother, Etienne, grew up with the stories of their native land that were continually repeated by parents who were anxious to make up for their children's sudden loss of their extended family and heritage.

From Priscilla, Nina learned of the poverty and injustice, the fear of violence and the horrendous environmental problems that caused famine and drought in South Africa. But she also saw wondrous pieces of native art and jewellery. Her imagination was stirred by tribal legends and beliefs. She heard stories of her childhood escapades in her family's garden, at the beach and on Table Mountain. She followed her parents' informed discussions of South African politics and picked up tidbits of news in letters from aunts, uncles and grandparents. When Nina died, she was wearing a T-shirt that bore the slogan, "Plant a tree for Africa."

Although Rocco and Priscilla left their country, rejecting its political system, they continue to respect many aspects of their South African heritage and take considerable pride in their family histories. Rocco traces his ancestry back to the earliest white settlement on the southern tip of Africa. The de Villiers family had been in South Africa since 1689, when three brothers arrived at the Cape of Good Hope, fleeing religious persecution in France and bringing their wine-making skills to the newly established Dutch colony. The family soon became absorbed into the dominant culture of the Dutch immigrants, who became known as Afrikaners as their own distinct language evolved.

Priscilla's mother was also a descendant of the earliest settlers, while her father's grandparents arrived in South Africa from Scotland in the 1880s. Priscilla's maternal grandfather was a commando at the age of 12 in the army which launched a guerrilla-style campaign in 1899 against the better armed British forces in the Boer War. When the Boers, as the Afrikaners were then known, were defeated in 1902, he went to school on a veterans' pension at the age of 14. He studied to become a veterinarian, and his subsequent career led him to the post of secretary of agriculture in the South African government. He was subsequently appointed as South African ambassador first to Canada and then to Australia.

In describing her grandfather's accomplishments, Priscilla spoke with great admiration about his intellectual prowess, his courage, toughness and initiative. Clearly, these were values that were cherished and nurtured in her home. Priscilla also proudly told me about her paternal grandmother, who survived the concentration camps established by the British during the Boer War, in which 27,000 women and children died. She shocked her Afrikaner family by marrying a British officer after the war. Her husband died a few years later but she insisted on sending their son, Priscilla's father, to a bilingual school where he learned English as well as the Afrikaans language that was spoken on the farms. Priscilla described her grandmother as a large, strong woman who worked as a midwife and would walk alone into the bush for as long as four days in order to give medical aid to African natives.

"Very, very strong people," Priscilla reiterated as she told me her grandparents' stories. She seemed to be summoning up from their memory the strength that she needed to speak eloquently of her daughter's death. She spoke of her father, who played rugby for South Africa before the Second World War in the days before the formidable reputation of the once proud team known as the Springboks was sullied in international opprobrium because of the country's racist laws. He appeared in a newspaper photograph assuming a fighting stance on the field with his fists raised after being fouled.

Priscilla told me that her father used to tease her by saying she always reminded him of a tank. Enjoying a joke at her own expense, she said some people assumed he was referring to her physical appearance, but in fact it was because he received a letter with the news of her birth while a tank rumbled by in the North African desert, where he was stationed during the Second World War.

Priscilla, her baby sister and her mother spent a year in Canada after the war, staying with her grandparents in Ottawa, where her grandfather was then South African ambassador. Her earliest memories are of Ottawa and the private school that she attended there. Priscilla grew up in the rarified atmosphere of senior military, government and diplomatic circles, as her father rose to the rank of lieutenant general and became chief of South Africa's defence force.

Although she grew up in a military family, Priscilla was never exposed to violence or racial tensions and hatred during her childhood and early teenage years. Her family was always kind and courteous to their black servants. Her parents and teachers at school talked with concern and compassion about extreme poverty and frequent famines among the African people. From an early age, she was instilled with the notion that it was her duty to help humanity.

Until she was 12 years old, Priscilla attended an art school run by an eccentric artist whose own abstract work was inspired by primitive rock paintings. He believed that only children were true artists and allowed them the freedom to experiment and have fun with huge pots of paint and big rolls of paper. Priscilla was infected with a love of colour and joy of creativity that remained a central force in her life.

A sharp contrast to the freedom of the art school was the authoritarian girls' school at which Priscilla and other white children were taught elitist but humanitarian values, handed down from the Victorian colonial era. There it was explained to Priscilla that she could not change her role as a white person who was better educated and economically advantaged. This was the luck of the draw. But she was told she had a duty to people who didn't enjoy the same privilege. The children were assigned simple practical tasks to reinforce this sense of duty. For example, every girl in the school had to knit a sweater each year, using new wool and taking care to do the job properly, and donate this sweater to underprivileged black children. Priscilla would later try to inculcate similar attitudes in her own children, who would never receive birthday or Christmas presents without first donating some of their old toys to a hospital.

While Priscilla grew up with an awareness of the suffering around her and a deeply ingrained sense of her duty to help, it was not until much later that she came to understand the problems in a political light. She was forced to confront South African political realities when she found herself reviled because her parents belonged to South Africa's ruling elite. She felt *she* had become the victim of prejudice, albeit on a miniscule scale compared to the systemic prejudice and intolerance suffered by black people in South Africa.

When she was 17 years old, she went with her family to England, where her father assumed the post as South African military attaché in London. They arrived in March 1960 just after an event which firmly established South Africa's status as the pariah of the international community. That event was the Sharpeville massacre, in which white police fired upon an unarmed crowd of black demonstrators, killing 67 people and injuring another 186. Priscilla was not even aware of the atrocity, which had occurred while she was sailing to England, cocooned in the luxury and old world charm of an ocean liner.

In England, she soon found herself verbally attacked by other students at classes she was taking to prepare for university admission. She struggled in vain to explain that not all white South Africans were cruel and inhumane people. She was continually harangued by young people for whom she was the only available representative of a hated regime.

For the rest of her life, Priscilla would have a fear and hatred of intolerance because of those false assumptions that were made about her. But she would also feel a deep conflict, as she did see her accusers' point that simply by living in an unjust system one was helping to perpetuate it.

When she returned to South Africa to attend university, Priscilla was forced to deal with the realities of the apartheid system, which maintained the political and social supremacy of the ruling white minority. She became active in a students' union which campaigned against segregation, learning political and organizational skills that she would turn to again as a middle-aged woman.

It was not easy, even for a white person, to agitate for change in

South Africa at that time. Priscilla had to tread a fine line between effectively fighting for her cause and going to jail for it. Eventually the students' union was banned by the government and several of its leaders were expelled from the country.

Some student radicals turned to violence and Priscilla was shocked by what she saw. She was horrified by a bombing at the Johannesburg train station. A young man put a bomb in a suitcase and asked an old woman to look after it for him. The woman was waiting at the station with her two young granddaughters, when the suitcase blew up. Later, a railway worker died in another bombing and police found dynamite in a cupboard in a university tutorial room. Frightened by these incidents and shocked by the callousness of their perpetrators, Priscilla diverted her political energies into social welfare issues and assumed a more nurturing role in helping individuals with their personal problems.

Priscilla met Rocco at a party attended while she was training for a job in the diplomatic corps, a job that she was destined never to take up, since the system did not look favorably on married female diplomats. Rocco, whom she married eight months after they met, was the son of an Afrikaner policeman and a woman from a family of English immigrants. He was born in Queenstown, an isolated small town in Cape Province about 200 kilometres inland from the coastal city of East London, his mother's home-town. Rocco's father was in his forties when he married, and retired from the police and moved the family to Pretoria while Rocco was still in his teens. With his father no longer earning a full salary, Rocco had to work from the age of 15 to help put himself through school. He spent a year in the army before becoming a medical student at Pretoria University. A shy, gentle man with a quirky sense of humour and a somewhat distracted manner, Rocco had a rigorous intellect and a consuming interest in medicine.

Priscilla lectured at a teachers' training college for two years after they were married, while Rocco completed his medical training. His interest gravitated towards neurosurgery and he obtained a post-graduate position at a surgery unit in Cape Town, which was reputedly the best in South Africa and world-renowned for its transplant operations.

The de Villiers would not, perhaps, have made the move to Cape Town were it not for a tragedy in their lives. Priscilla was pregnant and became very ill. She spent several months in hospital, much of the time immobilized and in great pain. Doctors believed that the twins she was carrying were alive, but they apparently died when she went into labour and were stillborn. Had the twins survived, economic considerations would probably have forced Rocco to put off plans for further training and begin working as a general practitioner. In the circumstances, however, they had no reason to stay in Pretoria and felt they needed a complete change.

Nina was born in Cape Town on September 7, 1971. She immediately resembled Rocco in looks, as she later did in personality. According to Priscilla, the physical similarity was so striking that one of Rocco's friends, who was visiting the hospital for the first time, identified Nina as Rocco's child out of six other babies in the maternity ward.

Nina was a precocious child who started speaking very early and soon demonstrated a somewhat stubborn spirit of independence, which was to be her life-long trait. She insisted on dressing herself and resisted any attempts to help her with many similar tasks. She began attending a play school when she was two-and-a-half years old, just before her brother, Etienne, was born.

Nina was also very musical. Rocco, whose parents had been well known in their community as amateur musicians, encouraged her to sing and play the piano. She showed an exceptional ability to play tunes that she heard on the radio. Priscilla was surprised to learn, however, that Nina did not like to sing at nursery school. She asked Nina about this and the child replied that it was because her ears heard the apparently discordant sounds that the other children were making.

While they were far from wealthy since Rocco was still studying, the de Villiers led a rich and happy life in Cape Town. They bought a small suburban home close to Rocco's hospital. His hours were long and Priscilla often took the children to meet him for tea in order to ensure that he spent some time with them. Like almost any white family in South Africa, they employed a black woman as a nanny and helper in the home.

Priscilla studied at an art school situated in the stables of a beautiful, rambling, historic house and it was there, she felt, that her art progressed from amateur to professional standards. She spent much of her free time painting and sketching outside and took the children, from the time that they were babies, in carry cots on excursions to the nearby slopes of Table Mountain. She also took them to the desert, which was a short drive away, and to the beaches on the shore of either the Atlantic or Indian oceans, both of which were within easy reach of their home. Often Rocco would join them at the beach after work and play with Nina in the sand or excite her precocious curiosity by pointing out crabs and other little creatures among the rocks.

As soon as he began to walk, Etienne followed his older sister everywhere. They spent hours together on the beach in winter and summer examining rock pools and looking for shells. Memories of idyllic days that the children spent on the beaches near Cape Town were kept alive for them through their parents' reminiscences as the children grew up in Canada.

The de Villiers' house in Cape Town had a small back yard covered in lush vegetation. Nina, who seemed almost undiscriminating in her love for all living things, would invariably choose to spend her time examining insects, chameleons, caterpillars, snails or slugs, rather than playing with toys. She would find little creatures in the garden and want to adopt them as pets. She would put them in boxes, jars or tins and take them into the house, giving them names like Basil, Katie or Reggie, after her favourite characters in the children's stories that Priscilla and Rocco read to her. Elizabeth Mbelu, whom Priscilla employed as a nanny and daily helper, refused to open a box or tin, for fear of finding insects or slimy creatures. Priscilla had to quietly go round the house after Nina had gone to bed and empty all the boxes into the garden.

The family owned a white poodle called Fifi who was Nina's constant companion and rode with her in her baby carriage. When she was four years old, Nina asked for a cat and her parents got her a Siamese named Bluebeard. This was soon joined by a stray cat, Tinkerbell, which the family found being stoned at the roadside by some children. Nina walked around wearing Bluebeard around her neck like a collar. One of Priscilla's treasured collections of photographs from those days showed Nina wearing Priscilla's frilly tennis panties with the cat tucked in the front of them and a tennis racquet cover on her head. She explained to Priscilla that she was being a kangaroo with a baby roo in her pouch.

In a busy thriving city like Cape Town and its affluent white suburbs, it was easier than most outsiders would imagine to distance oneself from the racial hatred, violence and injustice which defined South Africa in the eyes of the world. Priscilla remained socially conscious and concerned, but the harsher realities of South African politics did not impinge on her family during their first four years in Cape Town. She was engrossed with her children and peacefully content with the simple satisfactions of everyday life.

She had heard nothing about the political protests and riots which broke out in Cape Town in 1975 before she drove into the centre of the city one day with four-year-old Nina and the poodle in the car. Priscilla had her mind only on the banking and other errands that she had planned for the day. From the highway, she had noticed barricades on the city streets, but she assumed they were for roadworks. She was vaguely aware, but unconcerned, that the streets were crowded and the traffic slow, as she made her way into the business district.

A delivery van pulled up beside her. It was a hot day and her car windows were rolled down. Suddenly she realized that the driver of the van was yelling at her. He was a man of mixed race, who was therefore classified as "coloured" under the country's apartheid laws.

"Missis, get that baby on the floor, now," the man shouted, pointing frantically to the crowds of people on the street ahead of them.

Stunned, but comprehending the nature of the man's warning, Priscilla rolled up all her windows and put Nina on the floor at the back of the car. She told the child to hold Fifi and keep her quiet. Priscilla covered them both with a rug. She was afraid that a bark from the dog or even the sight of a pretty white child and a pampered-looking pet might provoke someone in the crowd which suddenly filled the street. Objects were being dropped onto the street from windows in the high buildings above. But on the street there was an eerie silence. African leaders had called for a silent protest. Priscilla was terrified by the sullen stares of the people who massed around her car as she edged slowly forward in the stifling heat, afraid to stop and unable to escape. A few blocks away, teenagers were throwing rocks and the protest was beginning to degenerate into a riot. When Priscilla finally did get through, she passed a phalanx of police dressed in riot gear emerging from large armoured cars and heading towards the crowd.

Priscilla was never physically harmed, but came close to being caught up in rioting three times and each time she had Nina with her. Although the riots became more widespread and more menacing, they never reached the suburb where the de Villiers lived. Priscilla was constantly worried, however, about Elizabeth, the nanny. Elizabeth was the mother of three children, whom she left with her parents during the day at her home in a black township outside Cape Town. Whenever the riots broke out, Elizabeth would race home to protect her family from the looting that raged in the township. On one occasion, her car was set on fire by the mob. Priscilla had always enjoyed a good relationship with her employee, but now she felt they were united by a bond that transcended race and economic class: they were both women struggling to protect their children from violent upheavals that they were powerless to prevent.

The third occasion on which Priscilla felt threatened by the rioting was the most terrifying. It was "Black September," a day when some black African leaders had reportedly urged that all white people should be killed. Priscilla was teaching at the high school when police called to tell them they should clear the school because rioters were advancing up the main street. Priscilla realized that Nina's school was also in the path of the riot, and as it was just a little university nursery school, police might not have thought of warning anybody there. Excusing herself from her duties at the high school, Priscilla jumped into the car and rushed to the school, where teachers were indeed oblivious of the impending danger.

Later that day, Priscilla was alone at home with her two children. Elizabeth had hurried home to her family and Rocco had been called in for emergency duty at the hospital, where beds had been cleared to await casualties. Telephones were not working and Priscilla could hear the sound of gunfire from the barricades a mile from her home.

Almost as disturbing to Priscilla as the fear of being attacked by rioters was the fact that many of her liberal friends and neighbours were themselves taking up arms. These were not renegades or fascists, but kind, gentle people, who cared about their black compatriots and did not support their country's racist policies. Yet they had purchased guns and walkie-talkies and were now out patrolling the neighbourhood in their cars in order to protect their families and their property. Overnight, what Priscilla had come to regard as a quiet, safe and peaceful neighbourhood had been transformed into something resembling as encampment under siege.

The situation seemed hopeless to Priscilla. She opposed the oppression that had provoked the riots, but she also knew that she would always be perceived as a legitimate target because she was a privileged white South African. She understood the motives of those who were threatening her life as well as those of her neighbours who were defending themselves. She abhorred the violence of both. Yet she knew that she too would kill, if necessary, to protect her own children.

Struggling with this dilemma, Priscilla realized that there was no future for her family in South Africa. She and Rocco decided to emigrate, but it was not a decision made easily. From a humanitarian point of view, they were aware that they would be taking valuable resources from the country if they left. As a doctor and a teacher, they could do much practical good in a society where most of the population was in desperate need of education and health care. And they had been happy in Cape Town. Their children were happy. They would be leaving close friends, family and a comfortable way of life.

But morally they could not support the apartheid system and Priscilla told Rocco, "I'm not prepared to have you or Etienne or anybody else going off to war to fight for this." They were repulsed by the violence and the threat of violence to which they had been exposed in their city and even in their neighbourhood. They were tired of being afraid for their children's safety. They were tired of feeling that they were powerless either to oppose the system or to protect themselves.

The de Villiers decided to move to a country where they not only could feel safe, but they could believe that they had a right to be safe. They chose Canada as a peaceful, law-abiding and democratic state which accepted people of many different races and cultures. It seemed like a place where there was no cause for hatred and little to fear.

Nina's life began in a violent country where she was well protected. It ended with an act of violence in a peaceful society where she should have been safe.

two

A PROTECTED
CHILDHOOD
IN CANADA

▼

N INA GREW UP feeling that she was valued and respected at
home and in her community. She was continually exposed
to stimulating influences and encouraged to engage in a wide range
of activities. Her talents were nurtured and her ideals reinforced.
She had a wide circle of friends who cared very much about her.
Many would be deeply affected by her death, which would be seen
by some as a violation and a betrayal of the values that Nina had
embodied.

"If I had another daughter, would I still foster in my child the
feelings of kindness and tolerance and trust?" asked Priscilla, as she
shared her memories of her family's early life in Canada.

She described Nina as a quiet, shy child who sometimes
seemed to be lost in her own world. Like other white children in
South Africa, Nina spent her early years in a sheltered and closely
supervised environment, well protected from the potential dangers
of a violent society. When they arrived in Canada, Priscilla continued to be a very protective parent. She worried that Nina might
not be alert to potential hazards around her or that someone might
take advantage of her generosity. She often feared that her daughter
might one day find reality too harsh.

Priscilla and Rocco were concerned parents who worked hard

from the moment they landed in Canada to provide a rich and stable environment for their children. It was not easy at first, since they emigrated with few possessions. Their funds had been frozen in South Africa and they had to establish a home from scratch on the small salary that Rocco earned as a resident at the Toronto Hospital for Sick Children.

When Rocco arrived, a few months ahead of the rest of the family, he found that the accommodation he had rented by mail was a shabby apartment in a run-down inner city neighbourhood. He knew that it was not an area in which Priscilla would want to send the children to school, so he frantically searched for somewhere more suitable. The only affordable family unit that he could find was in a large housing project in the north Toronto suburb of Victoria Park.

Nina was six-and-a-half years old and Etienne four when they arrived with Priscilla in April 1978. Priscilla was uneasy about how Nina would cope in the large open-concept class at the local public school. Nina did not like confusion and had been attending a small, structured private girls' school in Cape Town. Nevertheless, Nina attended and seemed to thrive with the dedicated, energetic teachers and children from a variety of different backgrounds.

She did not spend long at this school, as the family soon moved to another part of the city. Rocco rented a furnished house from a colleague who was going away on sabbatical. This was the first of several "sabbatical homes" rented for short periods of time while the family waited to establish landed immigrant status in Canada. The family eventually moved to Kingston, Ontario, where Rocco completed his training and assumed his first post as a fully qualified neurosurgeon.

Nina and Etienne became closer than ever during their early years in Canada. Etienne had always tended to follow his older sister around. But when he started school their roles shifted somewhat, since he was more outgoing and made friends more quickly than she. Nina began to depend more on Etienne, relying on him to test the waters first in any new situation. Even when she was in her late teens, Nina liked to take Etienne with her to parties and other social activities. Priscilla was concerned about Nina's shyness and enrolled her in various programs and activities in the hope of encouraging her to become more outgoing.

Although Priscilla continued to be protective, walking her kids to school long after other parents thought they were old enough to go alone, she and Rocco also treated Etienne and Nina in quite an adult way. The children often called their parents by their first names. Priscilla shared her opinions with them about serious issues as she told stories about life in South Africa. Rocco talked to them frequently about music and science, encouraging them to think for themselves and voice their own ideas.

Nina was placed in a program for gifted children while she was in third and fourth grades at her public school in Kingston. She gradually made some friends and enjoyed the company of the dogs and cats who came with each of the rented houses in which they lived during those two years. She began to study music seriously and joined an environmental club. When she was eight years old, she earnestly told her mother to start saving money. Nina explained that she might have to go to jail to protect the baby seals and that the money would be needed to bail her out.

In 1981, Rocco obtained a position at the McMaster University Medical Centre in Hamilton. This was a good teaching hospital in a large urban area and finally gave the family an opportunity to settle down and establish a more stable life in Canada. They bought a small house in Burlington, overlooking the bay in Lake Ontario. A few years later, they purchased a larger bay-front house in the same neighbourhood.

Nina was again enrolled in a public school program for gifted children. But at the end of her first year, the local school board scrapped the program under a new policy that involved integrating all children with special needs into regular classes. She was put in a regular grade seven class, although she had previously been working at a standard two grades higher. Priscilla was particularly upset to discover that this new class also included children with severe behavioural problems. Nina did not react well to the volatile atmosphere at school and became reclusive and depressed. The de Villiers decided to send both Nina and Etienne to a private school.

Hillfield-Strathallan College was the most prestigious independent school in the area. Its well-equipped, modern buildings occupied spacious grounds near the brow of the Niagara escarpment in the West Mountain area of Hamilton. It was a school to which members of Hamilton's ruling elite traditionally sent their children to be groomed for leadership roles. Here they were sheltered from the rougher aspects of life in a city whose wealth was made in the steel mills and other heavy industry that clustered around the polluted harbour. Its small classes, creative programs and reputation for academic excellence also made it the educational choice for many doctors, lawyers, university professors and other professionals who could afford to pay its fees.

There is no doubt that Hillfield provides its students with a privileged and protected environment. A teacher who spends much of his time counselling students told me that in 16 years at the school he had only witnessed one fist fight between students. Another teacher described Hillfield as an environment in which children from safe, pleasant and predictable middle-class homes, who expect to go to university and get reasonably good jobs, can realize their potential without being impeded by nastiness, violence or unpleasantness. In this environment, he said, the school was able to expose students to the values of a caring and civilized community with the hope that they would propagate these values in their future careers.

Almost immediately upon arrival, Nina began to flourish in the rich and structured environment that Hillfield provided. She soon became immersed in a variety of activities: sports, choirs, bands and, later, theatrical productions. Academically, she worked well in structured classroom settings, but also impressed teachers with her capacity to study alone and respond creatively to more open-ended learning situations.

Given a setting in which she felt secure and relaxed, Nina was quite a happy, spontaneous and adventurous child. She was brave and high spirited when she went sailing with Etienne in their little orange racing dinghy that Nina had named *Watamaraka* after an African goddess of evil. Years later, Etienne would proudly describe Nina clinging to a cord and leaning out over the water to keep the boat upright in a gale, struggling to keep her footing as the boat jumped over waves.

Nina's friends at Hillfield were like herself, somewhat reserved, intellectually precocious and on the fringe of the mainstream culture of the school. The members of this close-knit circle of friends would describe themselves as "geeks" or "nerds." They were kids who were comfortable with being regarded as weird by their classmates because they actually liked to talk about the subjects they studied and were less inclined to date and follow fashions. As they got older, the members of this group became far more socially and politically aware than most of their peers at Hillfield. Rather than spending their time at dances or clubs, they tended to meet at one another's homes to talk or watch science fiction videos.

To most adults Nina seemed extremely shy, but friends knew her to be witty, playful, argumentative and sometimes quite opinionated. A loud, ringing, infectious laugh and broad smile that seemed to fill her face were among the things that her friends remembered most clearly. They also remembered continually teasing her about her curly hair, which seemed to get more and more out of control as she grew older. Her friends were amused as they watched her struggle to free herself when she caught her hair in the sleeves of her school cardigan. They would joke that they could follow her tracks by the strands that she would leave behind her and, when something was lost, someone would invariably suggest looking in Nina's hair.

Nina seemed to enjoy being a little different from her peers and resisted the pressures to conform. But at the same time she liked to make an impression, often wearing striking make-up, colourful clothes and interesting jewellery purchased at craft shows. Sheila Singh, one of Nina's first friends at Hillfield, recalled that one Halloween all their friends had decided to go to a party dressed as 1950s prom queens with pony tails and frilly gowns. Nina showed up dressed in black, her body painted black, and with hideous rubber snakes springing from her hair. Sheila was dismayed and explained to Nina that everyone was going dressed as prom queens or princesses, but Nina was unconcerned and casually replied, "Oh, well, I'm Medusa."

She often seemed to her friends to be a little disconnected from the ordinary things that were happening around her. When Nina told Sheila about a family visit to South Africa at the age of 14, she talked about impressions and sensations rather than everyday events. Instead of telling Sheila that she visited her aunt and went to a game reserve, she said, "The grasses are very tall and the animals hide in the grass. The sky is very vast. Everything is much larger there than here."

Nina was often jokingly described by her friends as an "air head." They teased her about how she could be left in a corner and would sit smiling to herself for hours. But at the same time they all realized that Nina could be extraordinarily focused on school work and projects. She could be quite idealistic about a number of causes, but her idealism was frequently directed in practical ways. She was always highly organized about projects like running a Red Cross blood drive or selling chocolate bars to raise funds for a school in Africa. She liked to do things to help people and earned a reputation among her peers as a "stray dog person," because she often adopted other kids who seemed to be social misfits and tried to bring them into her circle of friends.

Many of Nina's friends sang and played with her in school choirs and bands. They all described her voice as having an ethereal quality. Her teachers observed that her attitude to singing was more intellectual and professional than that of most young people. She usually understood the music and was technically precise in her interpretation of it. Other members of the group tended to take their lead from her. She seemed at home with every style of music and created a stir in the school chapel one morning by appearing in a smart suit and tie with glitter in her hair to sing raunchy Billie Holliday songs with the school jazz band. Nina also composed quite sophisticated austere music in a modern style, but usually with a touch of quirky humour. One composition which included cacophonous percussion sounds was called "Walrus Falling Down the Staircase."

One of Nina's closest friends described her and her brother as "sickeningly well rounded." She also involved herself enthusiastically in several sports, particularly tennis. She enjoyed it immensely, although she was not naturally talented and had to work very hard to become a good player.

Although she was not competitive, Nina put a lot of pressure on herself to succeed at everything she attempted. When she did not pass her drivers test in her first attempt, she was devastated. It was the first time in her life that she had ever failed. A year later, when she got into an accident driving the wrong way down a one-way street in a snow storm, she was so hard on herself that the investigating police officer and the other driver were anxious to console her. Shortly before she died, Nina told Priscilla that she felt very relieved because in a few more weeks the demerit points that resulted from her accident would be expunged from her licence and she would again have a clean record.

Rocco and Priscilla did not overtly pressure their children to work hard and be successful. Those were expectations in a home where both parents put a premium on intellectual and artistic accomplishment. They were constantly stimulated and challenged by their parents' conversations. Priscilla often initiated long dissertations on many topics. The kids used to number their mother's standard speeches, teasing her by saying, "Oh, no, here comes speech number 733." Nina's friends loved listening to Priscilla, but also made fun of her tendency to expound at length. They called her "the wind goddess," after one particularly lengthy and authoritative explanation of the impact of wind directions on sailing techniques.

While she would sometimes enjoy an affectionate joke at her parents' expense, Nina seldom had any serious conflict with them. She could be stubborn when they tried to stop her from doing something she wanted to do. On such occasions, she would argue at length with Priscilla, but meekly accept a quiet, emphatic pronouncement from Rocco, who would say something like, "It's not appropriate. We don't do that."

Sometimes Nina would bristle with frustration, especially when there seemed to be any confusion or disorder in the home. She could be grumpy in the morning, which was not her best time of day, or tense and prickly when she came home from school. But she was generally contented at home and seldom quarrelled, even with her younger brother. She needed to spend a lot of time alone and appreciated being in a busy household where everyone was afforded his or her own space.

She would spend hours in her room reading everything from classics to trashy adventure novels. She loved science fiction and abstract ideas, but also wrote poetry. When she was just a 12-year-old, she wrote this poem, which appeared in her school yearbook.

> *The warm spring rain*
> *turns the snow beneath my boots*
> *to pools of icy slush*
> *The naked trees stand alone*
> *shivering in the wind*
> *which blows from the north*
> *to cut through my jacket*
> *chilling me to the bone.*
>
> *But if I listen carefully*
> *I can hear*
> *the insects hatching.*

Nina's early passion for searching out insects in the backyard led to an interest in gardening, which became one of the most important things in her life. When the family first moved into their home in Burlington, Nina set about clearing away weeds and planting shrubs. She also planted a lot of trees outside the house, after she and her friends obtained seedlings in order to help with local reforestation. Her environmental concerns led her to learn about composting and companion plants which would attract natural predators to control pests.

Rocco showed a great interest in Nina's garden and used to take her out to buy plants whenever he sensed that she was feeling depressed. On such occasions Priscilla used to tell Nina, "He spoils you." Nina would respond with an enigmatic smile and say, "I know."

Nina worked energetically in her garden but also spent hours dreaming there. Her family and friends marvelled at the length of time that she could spend sitting and watching a caterpillar eat a leaf. She would also spend a lot of time simply playing with her cat Shogun. It used to pain her, however, that Shogun was an excellent hunter and would often bring her prey into the house to toy with. Nina used to try to save these creatures and there were often a few cages around the house in which traumatized birds, mice and chipmunks would be receiving Nina's first aid treatment.

Ecology was one issue on which Nina was quite inflexible. When she visited South Africa at age 14, she was too shy to talk much with her relatives and too polite to voice any opinions about political issues. But she launched into a furious argument when she saw her aunt buying ivory at a game reserve. Her aunt explained to her that the ivory had been taken from animals who were being culled to preserve the herd and that the sale of ivory helped finance the reserve. Nina, who could even out-argue some of her teachers when she felt so inclined, replied that the sale of ivory gave value to that commodity and thus put the species in danger all over the world.

Pollution in the bay on which she loved to sail was a constant source of sorrow and frustration for Nina. Dead fishes would often wash up on the shore behind their home. From the tree-lined west side of the bay where they lived, the de Villiers could see the steel mills of Hamilton on the opposite shore belching flames and thick smoke into the air. It was easy to imagine the filthy effluent pouring into the water which also served as a harbour for heavy industry.

Nina used to fantasize about rowing a boat into the middle of the harbour and dropping seeds of the water hyacinth, a beautiful plant that can rapidly spread to cover bodies of fresh water with vegetation. This crazy scheme seemed to typify Nina to many of her friends, who consequently began calling her "an enviro-terrorist." It was also typical of Nina that what she actually did in response to her concern about water quality was hike to the perimetre of local landfill sites to collect samples of the run-off, which she then analyzed in her school lab, presenting the results at a local science fair.

Nina and her friends at Hillfield were regarded by teachers as an exceptionally bright and mature group of students who were able to work well together in creative projects. In grade 10, Nina and other students in a music class wrote and performed an opera called "Newfoundlife," based on a set of images and texts about Newfoundland. The following year, they started another ambitious project, this time in partnership with a group of art students. It was to be a multi-media production called "A Door is Ajar" and the idea was for students to create a world, inventing its customs, history and sociology, belief systems and art.

In inventing her world and its inhabitants, little creatures called Ninkians, Nina surprised her friends by thinking of details that nobody else considered. While her classmates were wondering how many heads or arms their creatures should have, Nina worked out welfare and medicare systems for her race and thought about ways to combat homelessness. Her friends never found out what the Ninkians actually looked like, but it almost seemed as if Nina had begun to believe in their existence. She and her partner in the project, an art student named Ian Parsons, used to bring cookies to class which, they explained, were Ninkian cookies.

One day, Priscilla accompanied Nina to the dress rehearsal of "A Door is Ajar," but parents and visitors were asked to wait outside while the students met in the theatre. While she was waiting, Priscilla was told the reason for this change of plan. Ian Parsons had been killed on the previous afternoon, run over by a car as he crossed the street on his way home from a rehearsal. The teachers had decided to cancel the public performances but had the students perform the piece one last time in dress rehearsal, in order to make a videotape that would be presented to Ian's parents as a memorial. Nina did not say a word when she joined Priscilla in the car after the rehearsal.

Later, Nina joined her friends, who clustered together to console one another. They attended the funeral at which three of Nina's best friends played the flute and other friends read poetry. The kids were dealing with something that made no sense in a world where their futures had seemed to be so clearly mapped out. "I never thought he wouldn't be there," Nina told Sheila.

Priscilla was disturbed by the state of shock that Nina still seemed to be in when she returned from the funeral. But Nina insisted on being private with her grief. Her mother became more worried and somewhat irritated as the silence continued for days. Priscilla took her for walks in the nearby Royal Botanical Gardens, where Nina usually felt at peace, but she still would not talk about it. Nine days after Ian's death, Priscilla and Nina went to the lilac dell at the gardens, where a brass ensemble was playing. Nina sat alone among the lilacs and listened to the music. Then she went for a long walk with her mother and talked about death.

They had talked about death several times before. When her cat died, Nina had been sad, but then asked everyone not to make a fuss because, she said, "It's nature's way." Nina understood that death was a part of the cycle of nature. She and her mother agreed that they thought cremation made most sense since it did not pollute the earth. Priscilla told Nina that when she died she would like to have her ashes strewn near the trails where they walked. She pointed out some of her favourite spots and Nina joked that she would never be able to remember where the places were.

Rocco used to describe Nina as radically agnostic, fanatical in defending her right to be undecided about religious questions. Nature was the bedrock of her belief system and it was nature that provided her with comfort and understanding in the face of death.

But the sudden loss of a friend and classmate in a road accident was hard to comprehend. Nature seemed to offer no explanation for this random death which had invaded the peace and predictability of Nina's world.

three

NINA'S
LAST DAYS

▼

N INA WAS SIMULTANEOUSLY a dreamer and a doer. She always
had a busy schedule of activities, but was also easily distracted. As a result, she was constantly rushing to keep up with herself.
In the summer of 1991, she was planning to buy a sail boat and she
told her parents she would name it *The White Rabbit*, after the
character in *Alice in Wonderland* whose refrain is "I'm late, I'm late
for a very important date."

Friends often teased Nina about her habitual tardiness and
teachers at school often noticed her rushing through corridors to
get to a class that had temporarily slipped her mind. When she
graduated from high school in 1990, a profile in the yearbook
described her as most likely to be found "in the wrong place at the
wrong time." No one could have anticipated the event that later
lent ominous significance to this light-hearted observation.

Nina did not like unfamiliar territory and it did not surprise
any of her friends when she chose to go to the university closest to
her home, although her high school grades were such that she
could have gained admission to almost any university. She loved
being at home and hated the idea of living in residence.

McMaster University was a good choice for Nina, since she was
considering a career in medicine and the McMaster Medical School
had an excellent reputation. It was a school that seemed particularly

suited to Nina's skills and work habits, because it emphasized self-directed learning.

Nina entered a first-year science program, selecting courses that allowed her to pursue an interest in genetics and biochemistry, which had developed out of her lifelong fascination with insects and plants. When she began university, she was still not sure whether she wanted to go into human genetics and medicine or stay in the more abstract field of plant genetics and pure science. Although she had been quite sociable during her high school years, she had always been happiest alone in her garden or in a lab looking at samples through a microscope. She felt nervous about dealing with people and was not sure whether she would be able to cope with medicine.

It was largely for this reason that Nina decided to do voluntary work at the hospital during her first year at university. She found that in fact she could handle the work and she liked being in the environment. Toward the end of the year, she was more firmly set on the idea of going on to medical school and Rocco encouraged her. He believed that she had the human sympathy desirable in a doctor, combined with the ability to remain objective and assess problems in a clinical fashion.

Priscilla was pleased that Nina seemed to have overcome some of the shyness she had shown throughout her teenage years. When Priscilla had an art show opening, Nina acted as hostess and showed genuine social skills. At school, she became bolder, voicing her opinions in class and talking to professors afterward. She showed that she was taking charge of her life by shopping or running errands that she would previously have refused to do alone. It seemed to Priscilla that her daughter was finally beginning to blossom.

Nina was establishing a reputation in Hamilton as an amateur singer. By the time she went to university, she was a member of two choirs. Although she did not have any conventional religious beliefs, she sang as a soloist at St. Paul's Presbyterian Church in downtown Hamilton. Just a week before she died, she sang in the church and the minister subsequently noted in a bulletin that he was impressed with how much Nina had matured as a singer and in her general demeanour and presence. Nina was involved in church activities and volunteered to contribute cakes to the church bake sale. Nina's friends in the church choir remembered the bake sale well, because Nina had stayed up most of the night baking and arrived at the church as the sale was ending. Her friends had to purchase all her goods.

Nina's social life still tended to revolve around her old friends from Hillfield. Several of them were also going to McMaster and others came home from university on weekends. Nina was still slow to make new friends and had no particular need to do so. She was busy during the week, commuting to school and studying. On weekends, she would usually get together with her close circle of friends. They tended to do things together in a group and Nina never had any particular boyfriend. She seldom discussed intimate emotional issues, even with her closest friends. Nina told Priscilla that she wouldn't be able to get on with all the things that she wanted to do if she had a boyfriend to worry about.

During their first year of university, Nina's circle of friends were just beginning to explore their role in a wider political and social sphere. Nina had always cared about the environment, but now she also became more concerned about social issues such as famine relief in Africa and violence against women. On what proved to be the only opportunity she ever had to vote in an election. Nina voted Progressive Conservative, much to the consternation of her left-wing friends.

In politics, as in nature, she tended to focus her attention on minute details rather than the broader scope. Nina loved to ferret out little nuggets of information to illustrate the inherent faults of bureaucratic systems. She would delight in telling her friends why systems fail and then link them to her philosophical beliefs about the mindlessness of humanity's attempts to control its environment.

Nina still liked to include Etienne in her social activities, though he was busy during the school year editing the 1991 Hillfield-Strathallan yearbook. He took a creative and innovative approach to this work and was full of enthusiasm for the final product when it was published in June 1991. He wrote an editorial comment at the beginning of the book which reflected an understanding of the world he and Nina shared:

> While you look through these pages, seeing many happy faces and recalling wonderful experiences, enjoy the moment, but remember that there is much suffering in the world. Kurdish children are running for their lives in Northern Iraq, suffering from exposure and famine. The black children in the South African townships walk barefoot to their schools made out of empty steel shipping containers, while political factions bicker and fight around them. The Irish kneecappings and the Johannesburg necklaces of fire decide the political and religious beliefs for the teenagers. At H.S.C., we ride to school on buses, and our attitudes are based upon what we see on the television and hear from our teachers, parents, and peers. We need not fear threats of death, torture or hunger.
>
> This book is not presented as a solution to world suffering, but as you witness the excitement and activity captured by the photographs in this book, remember that our carefree lifestyle is by no means common in our world.

Nina and Etienne enjoyed the company of their parents more than most young people of their age. Friends and acquaintances with teenaged children were surprised to note how often the de Villiers all went out together to dinner or a show. They were also all enthusiastic about tennis and sailing and spent time together at their racquet club and yacht club.

Sailing had always been a focal point in the de Villiers' lives in Burlington. In 1991, the family owned a 24-foot sail boat, and Nina and Rocco both talked about purchasing racing dinghies. On the last occasion Nina ever went sailing alone, Priscilla was nervous. There was a squall brewing and Nina, who had borrowed a dinghy from a friend, insisted on going out, even though Priscilla had warned her that she may not be strong enough to handle the boat. Nina was slight, five-feet five-inches tall, and weighed just 125 pounds. Priscilla asked the sailing instructor to keep a special eye on her. A dark cloud fell upon the bay as the boats were racing across the water. A dinghy that looked like Nina's lost its boom and its sail flapped uselessly in the wind. Priscilla became upset as she watched from the shore. Another little boat sailed over to rescue the disabled boat and to shepherd it to shore. Looking through binoculars, Priscilla saw that it was not Nina, but a very experienced sailor in the disabled boat and Nina was doing the rescuing. Priscilla later apologized to the sailing instructor for needlessly worrying about her daughter's strength and skill. She wondered whether she would ever stop feeling so protective of Nina.

The first week in August 1991 was a busy one for Nina. The family was getting ready for a trip to South Africa and she had volunteered to work at the Festival of Friends, a music and craft festival, which was organized by the father of her school friend Stefan Powell.

As usual, she was behind schedule and by Wednesday, just a week before they were due to leave, she still had a lot to do. She nevertheless spent several hours looking after a younger friend from the sailing school who had broken her collarbone while playing touch football. Nina took her friend to the hospital and stayed to comfort her over what seemed like a tragedy in her life, an injury which would prevent her from competing in a big sailing regatta in Kingston that weekend.

Later that day, Nina went to a photography studio to get a picture taken for her international driver's licence, which she would need in South Africa. Nina was disappointed with the photograph, which she felt was unflattering, and told her mother, "This is going to haunt me." Just a few days later, the photograph would be used on posters after Nina had gone missing.

On Friday, August 9, Nina was working as a volunteer at the Festival of Friends, which was held in a park in the east end of Hamilton. Her job was to keep track of the instruments that musicians left for safekeeping between performances. She enjoyed this job as it allowed her to meet the musicians, including some of Canada's most famous folk-singers. She was interested in comparing the actual appearance and behaviour of these stars with their media images.

One of Nina's closest friends, Chris Forrest, who organized the volunteers for the festival, joined her that afternoon in the instrument security area backstage. He was a former Hillfield student who also went to McMaster and sang with her in the St. Paul's choir. Nina was absorbed in conversation with Chris and Stefan, when she suddenly realized the time. She had to go to a shopping mall to pick up some things for her trip to South Africa and then to the tennis club, where she was due to fill in for somebody else in a club tournament. She told her friends that she was late and rushed off to her car.

After stopping at her house to pick up some jeans which needed to be altered, Nina drove to a shopping mall in Burlington, and left the jeans at a tailor. She stayed in the mall for nearly two hours and bought some underwear in a department store. According to store receipts collected and examined in a subsequent investigation, she made her last purchase at 8:34 p.m.

The Cedar Springs Racquet Club, where the de Villiers family played tennis, was located in a newly developed commercial area close to the Queen Elizabeth Way, the busy highway connecting

Toronto to the Niagara peninsula.

The racquet club was a large, plain building that accommodated numerous squash and covered tennis courts. Other developments in the immediate neighbourhood included several office buildings, a Holiday Inn, a Journey's End motel, a large restaurant called Jake's Boathouse and The Keg, a tavern and steak house. Also nearby was a garish Mexican-style tavern called Tequilla Willie's, which featured live music and had become very popular among a young, upscale crowd.

It never occurred to the de Villiers or other members of the racquet club that this was anything but a safe area. It was reasonably well travelled, with the hotel and taverns generating traffic in the evenings when the offices were closed. It was located in a suburban section of an affluent community that prided itself on having no serious social problems or crime. There was no reason for anyone to consider the danger of a strange man driving off the highway, carrying a rifle and a lifetime of problems from another world. No one had imagined that such a person might be cruising along the highway service road on the look-out for women whom he regarded as potential prey.

Nina arrived at the club expecting to play in a round robin tournament. When she got to the tennis courts, however, Nina discovered that she had made a mistake about the time of the game, which had been scheduled for earlier in the evening. Another woman had been asked to play in her place. This was particularly frustrating for Nina, not only because she had wanted to get some exercise, but also because she had arranged to meet her father at the club at 9:30 p.m. and drive him home.

A receptionist in the club talked to Nina at about 8:55 p.m. Nina told her about the miscommunication and asked if she could work out in the gym. She was informed that the gym was closed. She told the receptionist that she was supposed to meet her father and left her keys at the desk, saying that she thought she would go down to one of the courts and hit some balls on her own.

A few minutes later, another employee at the club saw Nina leaving the building dressed in shorts, T-shirt and running shoes, walking towards the service road and loosening up, apparently intending to go for a jog. It was not at all unusual for club members, men and women, to jog along the route on which Nina was setting out. It was a two-kilometre run around the large block on which the club was situated.

Nina was generally a cautious young woman. She would undoubtedly have been aware of the highly publicized murder of a teenaged girl who had disappeared in Burlington earlier that summer. But Leslie Mahaffy had disappeared in the early hours of the morning and there was no reason for Nina to relate that to her situation as she prepared to go for a jog before dark on a route along which she had often run before.

Dusk was approaching, but it was a warm summer evening and there were many people on the streets. Several of them subsequently reported that they had noticed the young woman jogging. By correlating these reports, police were later able to calculate that it took Nina about 12 minutes to complete one circuit of the two-kilometre block and that she set out for a second lap.

A rural couple who were spending their wedding anniversary at the Holiday Inn were leaving The Keg when Nina ran by. They asked her the way to Tequilla Willie's. The couple walked to the other tavern only to find that there was a long line up and that it seemed to be a younger crowd. They took a taxi back to Jake's Boathouse and noticed the same jogger in front of the Holiday Inn at 9:25 p.m.

Someone else had also noticed Nina. He was now watching her intently, waiting for his opportunity.

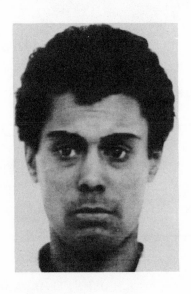

Part Two
JONATHAN

four

AN ANGRY
YOUTH

▼

JONATHAN CHRISTOPHER YEO often wondered who his parents were, where they came from or why they brought him into the world. He used to say that his father was black and his mother white. Sometimes he told people that his mother was Dutch, British or Italian. But the only thing that he really knew about her was that she had given him away.

He thought of himself as a piece of garbage, conceived by mistake and then discarded. This self-image was at the core of his personality, the driving force in an unhappy and brutally destructive life.

Jonathan learned early in life never to show his true feelings. He avoided getting close to anyone for fear of being rejected. He learned to be evasive and vague, but also to smile and be compliant. He accepted with gratitude whatever he received from the white adoptive parents who seemed to treat him as though he deserved second best.

For many years, Jonathan was able to make something of himself in the eyes of the world by being a responsible wage-earner and home-owner, the loving father of four children. Yet, secretly, he thought of his life as a façade. In a note found with his body after his death, he concluded that he was a cheap imitation of a human being, who did not deserve to be alive. He signed his name "Mr. Dirt."

Nobody in Jonathan's life seemed to care what he really felt about himself. But it became everyone's concern when he acted on his belief that he was worthless and allowed what he called his "animal side" full reign, unleashing his violent anger on the world. He became a cruel and cunning predator, beyond the understanding of anyone who tried to help him.

After his death, many people would think of him as a monster who should have been caged. What he did made it difficult for anybody not to hate him as much as he hated himself. Nor is it easy to understand him any better than he understood himself. Yet some light needs to be shed on Jonathan's life, not to explain or excuse his crimes, but to see how completely his problems were overlooked and the dangers that they presented ignored.

Jonathan once told a psychiatrist that the circumstances of his birth "left too much room for guessing." The same could be said of most of his life, since he was vague, evasive and uncommunicative. There are few details, anecdotes or loving portraits in Jonathan's life story, because nobody cared enough about him to record such observations, had there been any good times in his life. The people close to him had little insight and were more interested in themselves. If others had been more observant, more suspicious or more conscientious, his destructive behaviour might not have remained unchecked or his crimes undetected. Perhaps Nina de Villiers' life was lost partly because nobody cared about Jonathan Yeo.

One of the few things that Jonathan knew for sure about himself was that he was born in Hamilton, Ontario, on September 21, 1958. It was perhaps never clear to him whether he was a newborn or a one-year-old when he first entered the home of Mae and Raymond Yeo. He was always vague on this detail when asked to give a family history to medical staff or social workers.

This was a matter that also confused his younger adoptive brother, James Yeo, who told me that he had heard two different stories about it at home. He said he had heard that Jonathan came into the home when he was a year-and-a-half old but that his mother had also said that she got him straight from the hospital. James had also been told that Jonathan had to be sent back to the Children's Aid Society for a few months at some point.

I asked Mae Yeo, who declined to be interviewed in detail for this book, if she could clarify this matter. She told me that she received Jonathan as a foster child when he was four weeks old, but had to return him to the Children's Aid Society when he was one year old because she had cancer. She said she then took him back into her home three months later.

It is impossible to measure the impact that such a separation might have on a one-year-old baby and one can only guess whether there might have been other traumatic events associated with Jonathan being returned to Children's Aid Society custody. But it is well recognized by child psychiatrists that the bonds babies form during the first three years of life are crucial to their future development. Babies who feel abandoned or are badly hurt by their primary care-givers sometimes lose their capacity to love or trust anybody. These are the kids who grow up to be psychopaths — manipulative, often superficially charming, intensely selfish people, with an inner emptiness, an absence of compassion or conscience.

The feelings of abandonment associated with being separated from his foster mother perhaps helped to fuel the extreme anger that Jonathan harboured over being rejected by his natural mother. His insecurity about the circumstances of his birth was accentuated by the racism to which he was apparently exposed both outside and inside the home.

As a black child growing up in a white foster family, Jonathan was often subjected to racial taunts from other kids in the white working-class neighbourhoods where he lived. They would call him and his adopted brother, James, who was white, "Salt and Pepper." Sometimes they would use the nickname to refer to Jonathan alone, as he had Negroid features and light brown skin.

Jonathan was also subjected to racist comments at home, according to a woman who visited when Jonathan was a teenager. The woman testified at the inquest into Jonathan's death that she heard Mae make "crude and inappropriate" references to Jonathan, calling him "little chocolate boy" and "black baby." Jonathan believed that it was because he was black that the family had been slow to adopt him. Jonathan was not formally adopted until he was six years old, several years after the Yeos had adopted James, who was 15 months younger than Jonathan.

James, who grew up to be an eminently stable and congenial man, told me in an interview that he used to get preferential treatment in the Yeo household. He said he thought it had more to do with personality than with race since he always liked to have nice things, whereas his brother did not seem to care. One Christmas, James was given a brand new bike, while Jonathan received a second-hand one from a Goodwill store. But James observed that his brother seemed quite content with the present: "Maybe he thought, 'I'm lucky to be getting this.'"

They were both punished, however, with equal severity, James told me. Mae was always the one who administered discipline in the home and she was very strict with them, particularly when they were younger. She used to beat them with a belt, James said.

Clearly, it was Mae who ran the Yeo household. James described her as domineering, while he said his father was very quiet and liked to be left alone. Raymond was a painter at the Dofasco steel mills, while Mae was a homemaker who sometimes earned some money by babysitting. According to James, both parents were very withdrawn, tended to keep to themselves and were "not very family-oriented." He said his father was very uncomfortable with any social gatherings, while his mother couldn't be bothered to go out much, except to her Saturday night bingo sessions. Jonathan described his father as emotionally distant, while he told a social worker that his mother was "warm and someone you could talk to."

Jonathan and James drifted apart later in life as the differences in their personalities manifested themselves, but as children they had played together constantly. Occasionally, the family went camping and the boys fished and swam together. But most of the time they played in the city streets, where they would frequently get into fights and other kinds of mischief.

When I spoke with James and his wife, Laura, she told me that she believed James and Jonathan were allowed to "run wild" as children and were both "raised with no values." She said their family life seemed to be permeated with "back-stabbing and lies." She said that it was not until he left home that her husband was able to learn to manage his life or to love and care for another person. For years afterwards in their married life, she said, James struggled to overcome problems that seemed to result from his upbringing.

The instability of Jonathan and James' home life was exemplified by the number of houses they lived in and schools they attended. Most of the homes in which they lived were in roughly the same area of the city, older residential areas close to the industrial areas in the north-east section of Hamilton. They never stayed for very long in one house and always seemed to move far enough away each time for the boys to have to change school. Jonathan went to eight different elementary schools and two high schools. James could not, or would not, give any reason for these constant moves.

James coped better with new schools than Jonathan, who was cruelly teased and picked upon in each new situation. He reacted by withdrawing, keeping to himself and responding with suspicion and hostility to have overtures of friendship. This behaviour led to him being teased even more. He often stayed away from school and tried to earn status among his peers by playing class clown, which resulted in frequent detentions. Even if he eventually reached some familiarity with his new environment or established some positive contact with a teacher, it was soon time to move on to the next school.

On one of the rare occasions anyone in authority took note of Jonathan's problems, a school principal described him in a 1969 report as socially introverted. The principal noted that Jonathan had a problem in attending school and there was "a question in his mind concerning who he is. He is a brown-skinned boy adopted by white parents, with a white brother. Kids tease the nine-year-old brother about Jonathan being dark. He wishes he could stop fighting. He would like to be white. Says he's different from others 'because I have soft hair.'"

Jonathan's problems with self-image found expression in serious acts of vandalism, arson and assault. James joined him in these activities. On one occasion, they slashed the tires of all the cars in the parking lot of their apartment building. On another occasion, they burned down a garage near one of their homes in the east-end of Hamilton. When Jonathan was about 11 years old, he inflicted a vicious beating on a younger boy who had been bullying James at school. Jonathan approached the boy in downtown Hamilton after James had pointed him out, started a fight and, as James put it, "freaked out on him, punched him right out," leaving him lying on the sidewalk.

A few years later, James had grown bigger than Jonathan, who lost his role as his younger brother's protector. As a teenager, James continued to get into trouble on the streets and had minor brushes with the law. But Jonathan became more withdrawn, preferring to stay at home. He would spend hours in his room alone.

Jonathan joined the Navy League when he was about 11 years old and moved on two years later to become a Sea Cadet, encouraged by his adoptive father, who was himself involved in the Sea Cadets. These organizations have the goal of promoting leadership and citizenship. They train kids in seamanship and involve them in sports, bands and drills. Cadets learned to tie knots, fire rifles in target practice, dress neatly, polish their shoes and obey their superiors. Jonathan did these things well and worked his way up to the rank of petty officer in the organization. He played the glockenspiel and later the French horn in the band.

But Jonathan was not well liked and tended to remain a loner. Other cadets were wary of the volatile changes in his personality. He used to joke a lot and make people laugh, but would sometimes suddenly explode in a violent temper, getting into fights or throwing objects around. Just as suddenly, he would start smiling again, as if nothing had happened. A former cadet described one such tantrum during a band practice. She said Jonathan threw his hands in the air, banged his instrument on the ground and screamed at the conductor, "I don't have to do it."

At the two high schools Jonathan attended, he had average grades, though he felt intellectually inferior to other kids. He failed grades 9 and 11 English, but did well in mathematics, computer and technical courses and eventually graduated from grade 12. According to James, Jonathan made just one friend the whole time he was in school, although James could not remember who that friend was.

At home, Jonathan began drinking when he was 15 years old. He and James used to steal beer and cigarettes from their father, when he was out of the house on Saturday nights. Jonathan once described his father as having problems with alcohol, but James was never aware of any such problems. According to James, their father usually had a case of 12 beers in the fridge which would last him a week. But such moderate drinking habits do not seem consistent with the boys being able to raid his supply without him noticing.

Pornography was available and apparently accepted in the Yeo household. James said his father usually had a few magazines lying around the house, while Jonathan as a teenager kept his own collection in his room. Jonathan also used to go through magazines and cut out pictures of naked women. He spent a lot of time with his pornography and had no inhibition about masturbating in the presence of his younger brother, who shared a room with him earlier in their teenage years.

Jonathan also began taking drugs. On one occasion, he was picked up by police and taken to hospital as a result of a bad trip on LSD. When James asked him about taking the drug, Jonathan claimed that another kid had slipped it into his drink at school. James did not believe this and made some inquiries among his brother's classmates, who told him that Jonathan had taken the drug on his own.

Dishonesty and lack of trust was normal in the Yeo household, according to James. There were locks on all the bedroom doors and everyone in the family was careful to keep his or her possessions secure. It was not just because of Jonathan that James locked his door—he did not entirely trust his parents either.

James illustrated his brother's dishonesty by describing an occasion in their late teens when Jonathan took James's car without permission, badly damaged the rear end in an accident and left it parked outside the house so that James would think that someone had driven into it overnight and left the scene. James discovered the truth months later when he happened to be going through Jonathan's wallet and discovered two unpaid traffic violations relating to the accident. James had lost his licence because of the unpaid tickets. When confronted, Jonathan admitted what had really happened, and apologized in an evasive and half-hearted manner.

James quit school before Jonathan did and found a job in a steel mill. When he saw his younger brother earning money, Jonathan wanted to do the same and persuaded James to find him a job at his plant. When James later moved on to a better job, at Dofasco, where their father worked, Jonathan again wanted to follow suit. He submitted an application form at Dofasco, but did not make any follow-up phone calls or do anything else to actively solicit a job. James went to the personnel department on his behalf and secured an interview, after which Jonathan was offered a job.

It seemed to James that his brother had the same attitude to the working world that he had had as a child: he accepted whatever was handed to him, but did not have the confidence or the drive to push himself in any way. Jonathan was not prepared to take responsibility for his own life.

When he was 17, Jonathan joined the Argyle and Sutherland Highlanders, an army reserve regiment. He developed an interest in weapons and used to enjoy target practice with .22 calibre rifles at a range. He began to go out drinking in bars about four nights a week and had some money to spend for the first time in his life. He once described the social life of the militia as "a free-for-all." An acquaintance of his from that period described this social life in a newspaper interview with the *Hamilton Spectator* after Jonathan's death. She said, "They learned it was okay to drink. It was okay to be rough.... They all liked playing with guns. It was a turn-on."

In the organized activities of the Sea Cadets and the militia, Jonathan could feel that he was part of a group. But in his social life and at work, he still regarded himself as "a second-class citizen," a black youth in a predominantly white milieu. According to James, Jonathan was never the victim of overt racial prejudice, but was unpopular because he was often hostile and bad-tempered. Given Jonathan's personality and his reputation among his peers, it was not surprising that he did not have much success in dating. He could not cope with the snubs and rejections which are an inevitable element in teenagers' dating rituals. Whenever he was turned down, he became angry and more withdrawn. He responded with inordinate rage when one teenage girl, whom he dated for a few months, passed him up for another boy.

James, meanwhile, had a very active social life. He went out often and invariably had a date. Jonathan was jealous of his younger brother and was particularly envious of James's long-lasting friendship with Sandra, a young woman whom he met at Sea Cadets.

Sandra was 15 years old when she began going out with James and their relationship continued for two years until they split up in 1979. James did not hear about what happened after their separation until 13 years later — when Sandra and her mother Carol testified at the inquest into Jonathan's death.

▼

Sandra and her mother were among eight women who testified about being assaulted or terrorized by Jonathan. Each of them displayed courage in coming forward to speak of memories that still caused them pain, anguish and embarrassment. "I am hurting again," Sandra said as she recalled what had happened 13 years earlier. She told the inquest that she could think of nothing that could be done for victims to make them feel at ease, "sitting in front of a room full of people they don't know, spilling their guts."

The 44-day coroner's inquest explored all the events that led to Jonathan's death and to the murders of Nina de Villiers and Karen Marquis. The evidence of women who had been abused by Jonathan was crucial to this inquiry. The coroner had no power to make an order that the names of the victims not be published, but he asked the media to conceal the women's identities. Each victim who came forward testified under a letter of the alphabet. Sandra and Carol were Ms L and Ms P. Their first names have been changed here, too, since privacy is clearly important for these women and for other victims, who must be encouraged to come forward in similar situations.

Sandra's story about Jonathan showed that, by the age of 21, he had become a duplicitous and dangerous man. Something might have been done then to stop him if Sandra, like some of the victims who followed her, had not been too afraid or too embarrassed to tell her story.

Sandra, who appeared on the witness stand to be an insightful

and self-possessed woman, had been in a state of confusion and distress when she split up with James at the age of 17. For reasons
which she did not explain, the separation had precipitated some
conflict at home and she had moved out of her mother's house to
live with her aunt. While she was living there, she began receiving
phone calls from Jonathan, who claimed that he was interceding for
his brother in an attempt to get them back together again.

Sandra had known Jonathan for several years, as he had been in
the Sea Cadets at the same time as her, though in an older age
group. She subsequently saw him frequently, when she visited the
Yeo home and went camping with the family. She had observed
that Jonathan tended to separate himself from the other members of
the family and was usually excluded from their activities. She was
also aware of his outbursts of anger in Cadets, but felt that he generally conducted himself responsibly.

Jonathan's phone calls seemed, at first, to show nothing but concern and consideration for his brother. He told Sandra that James
really liked her and they should try to work things out together. As
the calls became more frequent, Sandra began to feel pressured and
harassed. She eventually told Jonathan that she would meet James in
order to tell him in person that there was no future for their relationship. Jonathan said he would pick her up at her aunt's house in a
residential area above the escarpment and drive her downtown for a
meeting with James.

It had not occurred to Sandra that she should be wary of
Jonathan. But she became uneasy about being alone with him in
the car when she noticed that they did not seem to be driving
directly downtown. He told her that he was taking a different route.
It seemed to Sandra that they were heading for the east-end of the
city, but it was dark and she quickly lost track of where they were.

Jonathan talked non-stop about how much Sandra was upsetting him and hurting him. He told her that he was 100 percent
behind his brother and convinced that she had to work things out

with him. Sandra was tired of hearing this and angrily told Jonathan that she had been hurt enough and did not want to deal with this issue anymore.

At this point, Jonathan pulled into a schoolyard and brought the car to a stop beside a baseball diamond. Sandra was apprehensive and demanded that Jonathan either take her to meet James or take her home. With a sudden movement, he leaned across and grabbed her arm with his left hand. As he did this, his other hand reached down into the space between the front seats and produced a knife. It was a hunting knife or boatswain's knife, similar to those used in Cadets for cutting rope. It had a six-inch blade and he held it to her throat. He told her, "If Jim can have you, I can have you too."

Sandra could feel the knife touching her skin. She was terrified, but she responded aggressively. She cursed herself for being so trusting and thought she would die if she did not act decisively. She told him, "You'd better make your first shot count, because my uncles are very protective."

Then she hit him under the chin with her fist and made a grab for the door handle. Jonathan suddenly appeared conciliatory and said, "Trust me. I'll take you back."

Sandra remembered shouting, "Screw you," and running away from the car. The events that followed became blurred in her memory and the account she gave at the inquest was confusing. She recalled reaching a store and milling around inside until she felt that it was safe to move on. She telephoned her mother at some point, but she did not remember where she was when she made that call. Her next memory was of being at a tavern in the east-end of Hamilton and seeing her mother there.

Carol, Sandra's mother, remembered receiving a phone call from her daughter at about 11 p.m. on November 15, 1979. Sandra seemed very distressed and asked her mother to meet her at the bar. Carol got the impression that Sandra was in danger and went there at once. She found her daughter engaged in a heated discussion with Jonathan and another young man who also was once in the Sea Cadets. How Jonathan came to be at the tavern was never explained. He may have followed Sandra there, or found her again by chance. Sandra testified at the inquest that she did not remember.

Carol recalled sitting with her daughter, Jonathan and the other young man for about half an hour without ever finding out any details of what had happened that night. But she saw that Jonathan was harassing Sandra. When Sandra said that she wanted to leave and asked the other youth to escort her, Carol decided to stay in the bar with Jonathan in order to ensure that he did not pursue them. She had, in the past, found Jonathan to be a personable, pleasant and respectful boy and she had no reason to suspect that he intended her any harm.

Jonathan was fidgeting and seemed to Carol to be "out of sorts." She knew from the earlier conversation that there had been some trouble that night, but she did not know what form it had taken. Jonathan began to get angry with Carol, complaining that she had been interfering in her daughter's relationship with James. Carol replied that she always spoke her mind with Sandra, but that her daughter made her own choices. Jonathan seemed to accept that explanation and calmed down. When they had finished their drinks, Carol said she was going to go home. She said she was very tired and feeling the effects of the three beers that she had drunk. Jonathan offered her a ride and she accepted.

As they walked towards his car in the parking lot behind the tavern, Jonathan suddenly turned on Carol, punched her several times and knocked her to the ground. He told her that he was going to get even with her and began kicking her in the face and in the ribs. Carol thought she heard someone come out of the tavern and shout, "What's going on?"

Jonathan ran to his car and drove away, but no one came to Carol's assistance. She was frightened that Jonathan would come after her again and ran off down an alleyway towards her brother's house, which was nearby. Her brother called the police, who took her to hospital where she received stitches to the inside of her mouth and forehead. Pieces of gravel from the parking lot had to be picked out of her forehead.

The policeman who took her to the hospital noted that she had been drinking and was moderately inebriated. He recorded her allegations, but told her that it was up to her to lay charges. Police policy in Hamilton at that time was such that charges would be laid only in cases of serious injuries, such as broken bones or deep cuts. In more recent years, almost all assaults are considered serious and the police lay charges.

Carol decided that she would pursue the matter and went to a justice of the peace to lay a charge of assault causing bodily harm. Jonathan was issued with a summons requiring him to attend the police station in order to be fingerprinted. The standard police procedure was that the fingerprints of a person accused of a crime would be kept permanently on record, irrespective of whether or not the accused was found guilty. The fingerprints on file and the information that accompanied them could be used in future to assist investigators, if the accused became involved in further crimes. In cases where there was no conviction in court, the fingerprints would serve as the only record that the accused person had come under suspicion for a particular crime. The prints could thus serve as a red flag to future investigators.

Jonathan failed to show up for fingerprinting and somehow this fact went unnoticed, although it is a criminal offence to disobey such a summons. This was the first of what was to be a long string of oversights and blunders, which resulted in police and other authorities failing for many years to recognize Jonathan as a danger to society.

Sandra was horrified when she heard what had happened to her mother. Sandra felt that it was her fault that Carol had been exposed to this attack. She felt intensely guilty, but too scared and ashamed to speak about it. She knew she should have warned her mother before leaving her with Jonathan in the bar. She then remembered that one of the last things Jonathan had said to her that night was "I'll make the bitch pay." Sandra knew that he was referring to her mother, because he had blamed Carol for ending Sandra's relationship with James.

At this point, Sandra felt that her mother had been abused enough already and it would only cause her more grief if she knew Jonathan had attacked her, too. She was afraid to tell anyone else about what had happened. Because she had not reported the attack immediately, Sandra did not want to go to the police; she felt sure they would not believe her. In fact, Sandra thought the police would more likely treat her as if *she* was the criminal.

Sandra had seen what had happened to her mother three years earlier, when Carol tried to lay charges against Sandra's stepfather. She had watched her mother suffer through a legal process in which she had become victimized again by the very people from whom she had been seeking help.

Sandra felt that it was better to keep quiet about what Jonathan had done to her. She was relieved that she had sustained only a few bruises on her arm. In her mind there was more chance of the court taking her mother's charges against Jonathan seriously, since Carol had had her substantial injuries documented by photographs, hospital records and police reports.

Years later, Sandra acknowledged on the witness stand that she might have been able to help her mother win her case if she had come forward with her allegations. But, as she explained at the inquest, "I was a scared kid and didn't know which way to turn."

Jonathan was found not guilty. Carol had been in such a state of confusion when she talked to police on the night of the assault that she had given them the name of the wrong tavern. She compounded her error by contacting them to correct her statement while her memory was still fuzzy, and sent them again to an incorrect location. The court was not impressed with a witness who was recorded in police notes as having been moderately inebriated and could not remember at which tavern the alleged assault had occurred. Jonathan denied hitting Carol. His lawyer suggested that she was drunk and had incurred her injuries by falling down in the parking lot.

Carol was so angry that she wanted to scream out in the courtroom. She told a police officer afterwards, "That youngster has gotten away with it and will hurt someone else one day. He's going to do it again."

Sandra was frightened that Jonathan would come after her, but she never saw him again. Jonathan's assault on her only came to light after his death and then as a result of a coincidence. As they prepared for the inquest, Ontario Provincial Police officers found out about the assault on Carol and set out to find her. They visited Sandra to ask her for her mother's address and she told them her story.

She was overwhelmed with guilt at the thought that she could have set a chain of events in motion that might have saved Nina de Villiers' life, had she said something to somebody at the time of the assault. She was also very angry when she learned that Jonathan's fingerprints were never taken and that so many other things would go unchecked as authorities continued to bungle subsequent investigations of Jonathan Yeo.

Sandra remembered how James and Jonathan used to boast about their exploits as children, about burning down buildings, slashing tires and beating people up. She recalled how they would brag that they could get away with anything.

five

ESCALATING
VIOLENCE

▼

THE FIRST IMPRESSION that Jonathan made on his future bride was not a favourable one. Sheila Yeo would later tell a social worker that she disliked Jonathan when they first met as fellow corporals in the militia in 1978. She was put off by the fact that he had no friends and she thought that he was "a jerk."

Physically, Jonathan was not unattractive. He was certainly better looking than he thought himself to be. He was a man of medium height — five-feet, eight-inches — with an athletic build. He had an engaging smile and dark, curly hair. He was able to charm people with polite manners, apparent sincerity and a good sense of humour. But there was often an intensity in his eyes which people found frightening, especially when his eyes were fixed in a cold stare or glazed over in a vacant gaze.

Although the more disturbing aspects of Jonathan's personality were the first things that Sheila noticed about him, she apparently set these perceptions aside. They began going out together soon after they met, entering into a courtship which would extend for two years and four months until their marriage on December 27, 1980.

Sheila was a heavy-set woman who was more intelligent and better educated than Jonathan. A middle-class family background had given her far superior social skills. Mental health professionals who subsequently dealt with the couple observed that Sheila appealed to Jonathan as someone who could organize and take control of his life. Laura, who was engaged to his brother, James, at that time, believed that Jonathan was attracted to Sheila because she had a domineering personality, similar to that of his adoptive mother.

At the same time, Jonathan also had a need to control and dominate women. It was while he was courting Sheila that he had become obsessed with his brother's ex-girlfriend Sandra and had assaulted her in November 1979. Jonathan apparently kept this, and many subsequent similar episodes, hidden from Sheila. The practice of seeking other outlets for his sadistic desires was something Jonathan seemed to build into his marriage from the very beginning.

There was little that Jonathan was ever reported to have said to indicate any love or appreciation for Sheila. In fact, he told his brother after their marriage that he did not love her and felt trapped.

Sheila did express love for Jonathan, but much of her love seemed grounded in his role as provider and father of her children. Sheila wanted to get away from her parents' home and dreamed of having her own family and a farm in the country. Perhaps Jonathan was willing to share her dreams because he seemed to have none of his own.

Sheila didn't seem to realize the gravity of Jonathan's problems and the dangers that they might pose until many years later when members of her own family were exposed to risk. It was because of Jonathan's assaults within Sheila's family that her mother would testify incognita at the inquest. Sheila's mother was referred to as Ms D, and I have chosen to use the pseudonym Nancy.

Nancy was an administrator with an organization that provided services to former prison inmates and people in conflict with the law. Nancy's work was one of the issues that had caused her to separate from her husband, an insurance adjuster, who did not share her values. Nancy had four sons and Sheila was her only daughter. Sheila's father made no secret of his opposition to her marrying Jonathan. Her mother had had some reservations. The family persuaded Sheila to put off her marriage until she completed a two-year community college course in social work.

Nancy testified that Jonathan showed impeccable manners whenever he visited his future in-laws. Nancy's first memory of Jonathan was that he was quite shy, soft-spoken, eager to know the rest of Sheila's family, but not forward about it. She said he was always attentive to Sheila and they seemed to be happy in one another's company.

Sheila's visits to Jonathan's home were evidently not as successful. In an interview with a social worker towards the end of Jonathan's life, Sheila recalled feeling uncomfortable and angry when she visited, because his father "had pornography all over the house — magazines and pictures on the wall."

After they were married, Sheila and Jonathan moved into a house in the small village of Fisherville about 45 kilometres south of Hamilton, near the shore of Lake Erie. Sheila had realized her ambition of living in the country, but this was to be their temporary home. Their long-range goal was to buy a property with more land. According to Sheila, they spent hours discussing their dreams of raising a large family on a hobby farm with horses and other animals. She admitted that this was her dream, but maintained that Jonathan had always shared it with her.

Jonathan had a well-paying semi-skilled job in the coke ovens at the Dofasco steel mill in Hamilton. He was in the water quality department, which controlled pollution in the effluent from the steel-making process before it was discharged into Burlington Bay. This was the job that James had helped him obtain. He never showed any initiative in trying to get a better job, although he came to hate his work. He was jealous when James was promoted to a job outside the coke ovens.

Initially, Jonathan's greatest regret about his new job was that his shift work forced him to leave the militia. He had had a good time and would miss the opportunity to shoot rifles at the firing range. He sometimes thought about joining a gun club so that he could get out to a range again, but he never got around to it.

According to his foreman at Dofasco, he was a responsible worker who did a very good job. His work habits, safety practices and attendance were all excellent. But his temper was so bad that his fellow workers used to complain and everyone hated to work with him.

One of his nicknames at work was "Nuts." People thought that he was crazy and would give him a wide berth. When something went wrong with the equipment with which Jonathan was working, he threw spectacular tantrums in which he would kick desks and doors or throw tools, hard hats and anything else in his way. A worker once saw him break the handle of a valve when he tried to turn it and then beat the valve furiously with a pipe wrench for about four minutes until it was totally destroyed.

Jonathan was also called "Zulu Warrior." His workmates maintained that there was no racist intent behind the name, which he acquired when he picked up an iron bar and used it like a spear to close a valve in a 50-foot-high tank of sulphur. These nicknames were only used behind his back, since, as one worker explained, "you wouldn't want a pipe wrench in the face."

His foreman also noted that Jonathan was very resentful of authority and did not like taking orders. He was a hard man to handle, the foreman said. "I could never really get through to him. I'd say "What's the matter?' He'd stare at me and say, 'I don't know.' He would shy away from a fight. I would ask him, 'Are there personal problems at home?' He'd clam right up. He'd never say anything. I always figured he had a problem, but I could never get to it."

Years later, when Jonathan finally found himself in trouble with the law, he would blame his problems on alcohol abuse, claiming that he lost control of his anger when he was drinking. But it appeared from his behaviour at work that he frequently lost his temper even when completely sober. His anger seemed to be triggered by frustration. He flew into a rage whenever he made a mistake or his equipment failed — whenever he could not control his environment.

The foreman was not aware of Jonathan having any problems with alcohol; nor were his workmates. In fact, Jonathan told one man with whom he worked that he was very much opposed to alcohol and also to pornography. He invited this man to his home for a visit. The man replied that he would drop by only if there was a beer in the fridge. But Jonathan said there was no alcohol allowed in his house.

When Sheila testified at the inquest into Jonathan's death, she presented a rosy picture of their early life together. She told the court that they did not have any problems in their marriage and that they spent a lot of time talking together. Although there were times when Jonathan had emotional difficulties and tended to pull away, they both cared very much about one another and their marriage bonds were strong, she said.

But Sheila evidently felt under attack at the inquest. Her testimony suggested that she scarcely had any idea that Jonathan had problems until the last few years of his life, when his outrageous acts could not possibly be ignored.

In an interview with a psychiatric social worker prior to Jonathan's death, however, Sheila did reveal that there were serious problems early in her marriage. She said that their relationship was initially difficult and that Jonathan preferred to spend his leisure time on his own. She said he "hardly talked at all and would sit in silence for a long time."

The social worker observed: "Ms Yeo assumed primary responsibility for the management of conflict and communication as well as identifying, discussing and resolving issues. However, the pattern of communication and management of emotions appears limited, controlled, constrained and inadequate."

Sheila told the social worker that conflicting attitudes to alcohol and drug use was one of the issues of contention between them. Before his marriage, Jonathan, by his own report, had been drinking heavily. Sheila maintained that she put a stop to that when they got married. She made it clear to him that she would not allow alcohol in the house. She said that she used to tell him, "No, we can't afford it. I don't think it's an appropriate thing to do. It isn't the way I was brought up."

However, Sheila did admit that she and Jonathan used to drink at parties. She acknowledged that Jonathan sometimes took drugs: marijuana, LSD and, on some occasions, cocaine. Jonathan once told a psychiatrist that he had a hard time relating to people and felt that he was only able to relate to alcoholics and drug addicts.

Pornography was another issue that caused conflict. When they were first married, Jonathan used to buy pornographic magazines and leave them lying around the house. Sheila threw them out, telling him that pornography is demeaning to women. But this was one area in which Sheila was unable to prevail upon Jonathan and the pornography kept appearing in the house. When their first daughter was born in 1984, Sheila told Jonathan that she was concerned that the child would grow up without self-respect if she was continually exposed to such material. Jonathan agreed to move all his pornography down to the basement.

Although the pornography itself did not involve any aberrant material and consisted mainly of pictures of naked women, Sheila was obviously disturbed by the use that Jonathan made of it. She told the social worker that he had an active fantasy life involving "women and what he wants to do with them." She did not explain exactly what these fantasies were, but left the social worker with the impression that the content was "sexually anomalous."

Jonathan's view of women and their role in marriage was chauvinistic and conservative to the point of being archaic. Jonathan attributed his beliefs to Roman Catholicism, though religion had never been a major element in his life. Catholicism was the religion of his adoptive home, but he and Sheila were married in a Presbyterian church. He told psychiatrists that he attended mass occasionally, but had also tried other religions.

He tended to split women into categories of good or bad, apparently seeing them either as "madonnas" or "whores." He respected and feared women like his adoptive mother and Sheila, who were both nurturing and strong. He believed that wives and mothers should play a subservient role in the home, caring for children and always ready to tend to their husbands' needs.

Other women he saw only as objects of his sexual desire — the "whores." In his fantasies, they were compliant and seductive like the women in the pornographic magazines, while in real life the women whom he pursued tended to reject him, as he believed his natural mother had done.

Jonathan apparently had no experience or understanding of any relationship based on equality or ordinary friendship. He once told a psychiatrist that he did not believe men and women could have platonic relationships. While he regarded women as sexual objects, sex was evil to him and linked with other dangerous desires. If he gave in to his sexual urges, he would also enter the world of his fantasies, which no doubt included a need to control and dominate. When women in the real world failed to conform to his simplistic pornographic fantasies and rejected his crude advances, he would respond with rage — not unlike that which he vented on tools and machinery that did not perform as he expected.

Sex with his wife was confusing and disturbing to Jonathan. Sheila believed in spontaneity in sexual activity and regarded sex as an expression of love within marriage. She thought it was fine for either partner to initiate sex and engage in foreplay. Jonathan was evidently threatened by these normal, healthy attitudes. He told a psychiatrist that he saw sex in marriage as a duty, carried out only for the purpose of procreation. He refused to have any sexual contact with his wife when she was pregnant and expressed the belief that "a wife should not want to have sex."

Jonathan was distressed when Sheila became pregnant with their first child about three years after they got married. He burst into tears when he told James and Laura, and said he did not want a child and that Sheila had tricked him.

It was not clear from the evidence at the inquest whether it was before or after Sheila became pregnant that Jonathan began to force his attentions on his next victim. When Janet K testified, she was somewhat confused about the dates of events she had long been trying to forget. But it is certain that Jonathan terrorized this young woman for several months and the last in the series of incidents was recorded in a police officer's notes on May 30, 1984, just over two weeks after the Yeos' first daughter was born.

Janet was a short, dark-haired young woman who appeared at the inquest conservatively dressed in a white blouse and red plaid jacket. In 1983, she was a single working woman who lived alone in Hamilton. Her social activities were mostly limited to visiting her parents and girlfriends after work and playing once a week in a ten-pin bowling league. It was there that she met Jonathan and Sheila, who bowled regularly in the early years of their marriage. Janet was friendly and sociable with them, as with the other people who played in the league and got together for drinks afterwards. She had no particular relationship with Jonathan and did nothing that she was aware of to trigger his interest in her. She had no idea that he even knew where she lived, until he showed up one day on her doorstep.

She assumed at the time that he must have been passing by and recognized her car parked in front of her home. In retrospect, it would seem more likely that he had been stalking her on previous occasions and had followed her home. But at the time, Janet accepted Jonathan's story that he was on his way to work and thought he would ask if he could use her phone because he needed to call Sheila. As other women would learn, Jonathan had a gift for making preposterous stories seem plausible.

While his approach had been bizarre, Jonathan conducted himself properly on his first visit to Janet's home, a downstairs apartment in an older house. He subsequently dropped in a few more times, saying he was on his way to work and had time to kill. Janet made him coffee and they talked. On one of these occasions, Jonathan had a glazed look in his eyes and offered Janet some pills, which she refused.

Eventually, Jonathan asked Janet if she was going out with anybody and invited her out on a date. She said that she did not get involved with married men. Jonathan told her that he had separated from his wife and Janet replied, "I still don't get involved with married men."

Janet went to visit a girlfriend after work one evening and arrived home at about 11:30 p.m. She was unlocking her apartment door and had not yet closed the outer door of the house, when she realized that she was not alone. Jonathan was standing behind her in the lobby. She was terrified, especially as she had no idea how he got there. His car had not been parked outside the house.

Jonathan asked her where she had been and Janet replied, "It's none of your business."

When Jonathan asked her to invite him in for coffee, Janet said it was too late and that she was going to bed.

"That's fine. We'll go together," said Jonathan.

Janet responded with an indignant, "No." But she had already unlocked the door before Jonathan had appeared. He pushed it open and walked into the apartment.

Nervously attempting to take control of the situation, Janet told Jonathan that she would make him some coffee and that he would have to leave after he had drunk it. She walked into the kitchen and he followed her. As she was getting the coffee cups out, Jonathan put his hand on her shoulder and tried to kiss her. She turned her head away and said, "You're leaving. Get out."

Jonathan refused to leave and continued to press himself upon her. He tried to kiss her again and Janet kneed him in the groin. There was a knife nearby on the kitchen table. Jonathan grabbed it and held it to Janet's throat. He told her, "You'll be sorry."

In the tense silence which followed this threat, Janet heard footsteps in the upstairs apartment. She knew that her neighbour Jim was home. She told Jonathan that she would start screaming unless he left at once and that Jim would come to her aid. Jonathan did not say a word, but put down the knife and walked out of the apartment.

Janet ran to the door and locked it after him. Then she made sure that all her curtains were closed. Still terrified, she went into the bathroom to hide. In retrospect, it did not make any sense to her that she shut herself in the bathroom, when she knew that Jonathan was safely out of the apartment. It would have been more sensible to have called for help. But, she explained at the inquest, "I was so scared. I didn't think to call. I just wanted to hide and not come out."

A few days later, Jonathan phoned and apologized profusely for his behaviour. Janet responded, "Fine, apology accepted. I don't want to see you. I don't want you to come to my house anymore."

However, Jonathan continued to harass her. He called again and she hung up the phone as soon as she heard his voice. He kept on calling her and she began unplugging her phone or leaving it off the hook for long periods. But it seemed that almost any time she reconnected it, he would be on the line again. Janet decided that the only solution was to get a new, unlisted number.

Jonathan returned to Janet's house one day when she was out. She arrived home to find him in the lobby talking to her neighbour Jim. Jonathan asked Janet if she would invite him in for a coffee and she told him that he was to leave. She said that she never wanted to see him again. After he left she told Jim that Jonathan had been harassing her. Jim said he would send him away if he showed up again and that she should call him if she had anymore problems.

Janet did not say anything to her friends in the bowling league because they were also Jonathan's friends and she feared that they might not believe her. She just ignored Jonathan if she saw him at the bowling lanes. She always refused invitations to socialize with her friends afterwards because she was afraid that he might join them.

Fear of another attack forced Janet to change her routines. She was cautious about going home at night and constantly afraid that she would find him again on her doorstep. She tried to vary the time at which she arrived home by spending more time with her friends or her parents after work.

One morning in the spring, Janet went home after working a night shift. She noticed nothing untoward and went straight to bed. At about 10:30 a.m., she got up to go to the bathroom and heard a noise in her room. As she paused to listen, her bedroom closet opened and Jonathan walked out.

Janet screamed and her first instinct was to try to cover herself with her housecoat. Jonathan snatched it from her, saying, "You won't be needing that."

She managed to break away from him and ran through the apartment to the front door. She got the deadbolt undone before he caught up with her and grabbed her arm. Believing that her best defence lay in making as much noise as she could, Janet continued to scream loudly and yell at Jonathan, telling him to get out of the house at once. But this time her neighbour was not home. It occurred to Janet afterwards that Jonathan had probably checked to make sure Jim was at work before breaking into the apartment.

Janet continued to struggle with the door and got into the lobby of the house, while Jonathan tried to persuade her that he was not going to hurt her, that she should calm down and everything would be okay. Jonathan was perhaps afraid that her screaming would attract attention or felt intimidated by the fury of her resistance. It is also possible that Jonathan's own better self prevailed and that he actually believed what he was saying as he tried to assure her that he would never do anything to harm her. For whatever reason, Jonathan did in fact leave without inflicting any further harm.

Now Janet was completely terrified. She was convinced that Jonathan was capable of raping or murdering her. Yet she was still reluctant to call the police. She phoned her father and told him that a man from the bowling alley was bugging her and had broken into her apartment. Her father came to her house immediately and secured all the windows. Janet discovered that Jonathan had entered through a window that had not been properly fastened.

Like many female victims of male violence, Janet did not want her parents to know the details. She felt she could not talk to her father about intimate matters. It was hard to explain or even think about the kind of emotional pain and fear that Jonathan had caused her.

Janet was also reluctant to identify Jonathan to her father. She was afraid that he would either go to the police or take the law into his own hands. She simply told him that her stalker frequented the bowling alley, drove a red Honda and his first name was Jon. In fact, Janet learned later that her father did go to the bowling alley looking for Jonathan, but did not find him.

Janet's father later told her that he had contacted the police, who informed him that they could do nothing unless the man who was harassing his daughter actually harmed her. Although she could hardly have been reassured by this, Janet was relieved that the police would not get involved. She explained at the inquest that she had not called them herself because of what she had heard through the media about what happened to other women who were attacked: "You always seem to be accused of being at fault, regardless of whether you are or not." She also feared that her judgement — and even her motives — might be questioned, especially since she had failed to report the previous assault.

Jonathan began phoning Janet again. He had apparently discovered her unlisted number when he broke into the apartment, but he told Janet that he found out her number through a friend at the phone company. He wanted to make her feel that he had power and influence, that she could not hide from him. She began unplugging her phone again, but this made her feel more vulnerable as it would not be available in an emergency. She imagined herself having to fumble with the phone jack while Jonathan was coming after her.

On May 29, 1984, Janet received a call from Jonathan. He said he wanted to talk to her and was going to drop in at her apartment. Janet told him that she did not want him to visit and that she would call the police if he came. He replied, "I'll break your front window. I'll kill you if you call the cops."

After she went to bed that night she heard a noise outside her door. It sounded as if there was someone in the lobby between the apartment door and the outer door of the house, which was always kept locked. She shouted, "Who's there?" and Jonathan's voice responded, "It's me."

"I'm going to call the police," said Janet, as she checked to make sure that her apartment door was firmly locked.

"Yeah, you always say that," Jonathan replied and began to pound his fist against the door.

Janet phoned the police, reporting that a man had broken into the house and was banging at her apartment door. She was asked if she knew the man and she replied that she did. She was told that an officer would be dispatched immediately.

Jonathan was nowhere in sight when a police officer arrived about five minutes later. Janet told the police officer very little about the previous incidents. At the inquest, she explained, "I was scared and I didn't want to let my family know all the details. I was scared to tell anyone else. I wanted it to end. I figured if I told the police it would continue. I was hopeful that after I called the police, Jonathan was going to understand that I wasn't going to put up with him anymore."

The police officer got the impression from Janet that the suspect in this case was an estranged boyfriend. He had no reason to believe it was anything other than a routine call. He personally handled about 15 to 20 cases a month involving ex-spouses or boyfriends harassing their former partners. The officer told Janet that she could lay a charge before a justice of the peace within 48 hours, but he felt sure that she would not do so. Women seldom bothered to lay such charges in those days and these so-called "domestic" cases were not given high priority by the police force. Nevertheless, the officer did take the matter seriously enough to park his car outside the house for the remainder of his shift.

Janet gave the police officer Jonathan's name and told him where he lived. The officer was to do a routine check to see if the name appeared on police records. There was, of course, no record, because someone had forgotten to ensure that Jonathan showed up for fingerprinting when he was charged in 1979. If there had been a record to show that Jonathan had been involved in another violent incident, even though he was acquitted, the police officer might have taken Janet's complaint more seriously. As it was, no one bothered to do a follow-up investigation. The police officer involved told the inquest, "I have no idea why I didn't pursue it."

Jonathan did not harass Janet anymore, though she did see him a year later outside her apartment. She was married by this time and she was just on her way out with her husband when Jonathan emerged from her backyard. She asked him what he was doing there. He looked at her and then at her husband, apparently surprised that she had a man in the house. He stared at them silently for a moment, turned and walked away.

Janet saw or heard nothing more of him until she heard the news of his death and of the crimes that he was alleged to have committed. One of her friends said that it was hard to believe that the murderer of Nina de Villiers and Karen Marquis was the same mild-mannered man who used to go bowling with them. But Janet later told her husband, "That was the same Jonathan Yeo that I knew."

six

A FAMILY
CLOSES RANKS

▼

SHEILA KNEW THAT Jonathan was distressed and confused during
the time that she was pregnant with their first child. She sensed
that he was pulling away from her. But she did not know what was
really happening with him. It was not until later that she was forced
to recognize that her husband was dangerously disturbed. When she
was eventually confronted with alarming evidence, she responded
in ways which led many people to believe that she stood by and
allowed Jonathan to continue unchecked along his increasingly
destructive course.

At the subsequent inquest into Jonathan's death, Sheila's lawyer,
Raymond Harris, maintained that his client was cast as a scapegoat.
He complained that Sheila was unnecessarily castigated in court and
pilloried in the media. Even her physical appearance was unfairly
represented, said Harris, who took exception to television news
reports in which unflattering video footage and courtroom sketches
made her look "like a seasoned biker."

In the eyes of Sheila's friends and family, she simply did what
any spouse might be expected to do. She stood by her husband,
tried to protect him and struggled to keep her family together.
When she found herself confronted with problems that were too
complex for her to handle, she looked for help in the community,
but could not find any. Sheila's mother, Nancy, complained at the

inquest, "I think I'm being asked — and women in the family are being asked — to accept responsibility for feeling, treating and caring for someone whose problems, we've now been told, were beyond being helped or treated."

It is not easy to say where family loyalties end and public duty begins. It is even harder to recognize when one must give up protecting someone one loves. These were the difficult choices Sheila and her family faced. It was perhaps only in hindsight that they were able to see that other people's lives depended on the choices that they made.

With the benefit of hindsight, it might seem that Jonathan's conviction in 1985 for possession of an unregistered restricted weapon would be seen as a dangerous precedent. However, this was a crime that even the police did not seem to take very seriously. It involved a starter's pistol that had been altered in order to fire live ammunition. Police found it in the Yeos' kitchen in a drug raid on their home in August 1984. The police also discovered 56 marijuana plants in seeding boxes in a shed behind the house. Jonathan was arrested and charged in connection with both the drugs and the firearm. The drug charge was dropped when Sheila claimed responsibility for the plants and pleaded guilty in court to cultivation of marijuana.

Police were not particularly concerned about the starter's pistol, because it was found that it did not work, even though it had been altered with the clear intention of converting it into a weapon. Jonathan claimed he found it in a paper bag on a street corner on his way home from work, took it home, discovered it did not work, put it away in a drawer and forgot about it. Sheila said that she told Jonathan to throw it away because she did not want a gun in the house. She had assumed that he obeyed her. In February 1985, Jonathan was fined $100, put on probation for 12 months and prohibited from possessing a firearm for three years. He now had a criminal record and his fingerprints would be available for use in future investigations.

In December 1985, Jonathan and Sheila moved into a farm house with 10 acres of land near the village of Caistor Centre on the Niagara escarpment about 30 kilometres south-east of Hamilton. They bought a horse and began to work on improving the property. Jonathan worked with furious energy digging a pond, building fences and renovating the house and outbuildings. Occasionally, he flew into a temper when he did not have the right tools for the job or when supplies failed to arrive. But according to Sheila and her family, he was a good father to his child and seemed happy when a second daughter arrived in September 1986.

Sheila's mother, Nancy, stayed with them for eight months in 1986. She gave a glowing account, when she testified at the inquest, of Jonathan's treatment of his children: "Jonathan was unquestionably ecstatic to have children. He was extremely attentive to those new little bits of humanity that came into the family. He never left or came into the house without addressing each one. He kissed them, played with them — sometimes I felt more than he needed to — dressed them, bathed them and looked after them."

When she lived with Sheila and Jonathan, Nancy said she had "a great sense of a couple building something together that both of them wanted. They seemed to be pleased with what they were doing." She explained that Sheila suffered from allergies and Jonathan therefore did a lot of the housework, in addition to remodelling parts of the house and working long hours at the steel mill. But Jonathan never balked at doing extra work and seemed to enjoy it, according to Nancy, who observed, "They loved each other very much. They were devoted to each other."

Sheila and Nancy got the impression that Jonathan liked Sheila's family and enjoyed their company, perhaps more than his own family. He seemed to enjoy an excellent relationship with his mother-in-law. That made what happened in March 1987 all the more incomprehensible.

Nancy, who had moved into an apartment building in Hamilton, arrived home from work at about 5:30 p.m. on March 27, 1987. When she tried to switch the lights on in her seventh-storey apartment, Nancy found that none of them would work. She left the apartment to try to find out if the power was off in the whole building. As she walked along the corridor, Jonathan appeared from behind a fire door. She had not been expecting him and was surprised to see him emerge from a fire escape. But she had no particular reason to be concerned as she took him into her apartment and explained that the lights were off. Jonathan then told her that he had come into the apartment earlier and turned all the lights off at the fuse panel. While he restored the power by screwing the fuses back into place, Nancy asked him for an explanation.

Jonathan told her that he had been drinking at a nearby bar and had become involved in a fight. He said he had hurt somebody and went to hide in Nancy's apartment because he was scared.

When she heard his story, Nancy thought it would be a good idea to call a friend of hers for advice. But Jonathan did not want her to use the phone and physically restrained her from doing so. He began to pace up and down the entire length of the apartment, walking into each of the rooms. He looked unkempt and had obviously been drinking. He was carrying an open bottle of rye whiskey.

As Nancy stood still, listening to Jonathan pace and wondering what to do, he came up behind her. She felt his hands on her neck and stiffened with shock as his fingers pressed on her throat. She was confused, unable to comprehend what was happening. For a moment she relaxed, assuming that he must be teasing or fooling around. But the pressure on her neck increased. She could not think why he would be doing such a thing. He continued to press harder and it became more and more difficult for her to breathe. There was little doubt that Jonathan was trying to strangle her.

As she fought for breath, Nancy managed to whisper,

"Jonathan, you're hurting me. Jonathan, you're going to hurt Sheila and the children. Jonathan, please don't do this. Sheila loves you. Please don't do this."

Releasing his grip, Jonathan turned his head away and began to cry. He told Nancy that he did not mean to hurt her. He was standing beside a glass door which opened onto a balcony. The door was closed but Jonathan suddenly lunged into it, saying, "I'm getting out of here." He hit the door with such force that the glass broke and his arm was cut quite badly. Jonathan looked surprised, as if puzzled by what he had done, and went to the bathroom to wash off the blood.

Nancy took advantage of his absence to make the phone call that she had tried to make earlier. She asked her friend, a minister, to come to her assistance. When he arrived ten minutes later, Jonathan was still in the bathroom. They persuaded him to come out and the minister tried to calm him down. But Jonathan ran out of the apartment, apparently still in a demented state. They decided that it would be best to call the police for Jonathan's own protection.

They told the police that Jonathan had tried to jump through the window of the seventh-storey apartment, but they did not mention that he had tried to kill Nancy. Nancy explained at the inquest that she could not believe at the time that Jonathan had any criminal intent. Although she realized that Jonathan had tried to strangle her, Nancy said that she did not see this as a deliberate attempt on her life. She said, "I thought, this is my son-in-law and he has a problem and he needs help."

Two police officers responded quickly to Nancy's call and, with the help of her friend, found Jonathan on the street. When they approached him, he fell to the ground, saying that he wanted to die and join God. They apprehended him under the Ontario Mental Health Act, which gives police the power to take people to a hospital for psychiatric examination if they seem to be acting insanely and appear dangerous to themselves or others. After leaving Jonathan for overnight observation at St. Joseph's Hospital in Hamilton, the officers made an entry onto computerized police records to indicate to anyone dealing with him in future that he may be suicidal. At the inquest, the police officers said that they would certainly have charged Jonathan with a criminal offence if they had known about the attack on Nancy.

Jonathan was examined by psychiatrists and released the following morning. The psychiatric staff at the hospital had not been told about the assault. They had no idea that they were dealing with anything other than a clumsy suicidal gesture by a drunken man. If they had known that they were dealing with someone who had shown a murderous rage against a family member whom he ostensibly loved, they might have examined and treated Jonathan differently. Psychiatrists base part of their diagnosis on the information that they are given about a patient's past behavioural history. Nancy had decided not to tell police about the assault because she wanted Jonathan to get psychiatric help. But her decision to withhold that information also inhibited any effective psychiatric intervention at the hospital.

When Sheila subsequently talked to Jonathan about the incident, he said that he had been drinking that night and did not remember what happened. He told Sheila that he was shocked and upset because he cared deeply about Nancy. They went to visit Nancy a few days after the incident and, according to Nancy's tearful testimony at the inquest, Jonathan said, "We've come because I want to apologize to you for hurting you the other night. I don't know why I did that. You've been a great mother-in-law to me and I have no reason to hurt you."

When Nancy urged Jonathan to seek psychiatric help, he and Sheila both agreed that they would do so. Sheila assured her mother that Jonathan had never hurt or threatened her or the children. She promised Nancy that she would tell her if she ever felt that she or her children were at risk.

They did seek psychiatric help for Jonathan, but found that the regional organization of health care services required that he go to a hospital in St. Catharines, 45 kilometres east of his home, rather than in Hamilton, which was where he worked and closer to his home. Perhaps the inconvenience of driving to St. Catharines for therapy contributed to Jonathan's failure to take full advantage of services offered to him there.

At St. Catharines General Hospital, staff were made aware that Jonathan had tried to strangle his mother-in-law and had inflicted harm on himself. He explained that he was driven by an explosive rage that built up over minor incidents at home. He told a psychiatrist that he got angry when his children were whining, when someone banged into the table, dropped something on the floor or even changed the subject during a conversation. He sometimes felt like ending his life, he said, by "going down to the garage and going for a long, long drive."

It was clear to hospital staff that Jonathan was deeply troubled and that his behaviour caused serious concerns. But he was not found to be suffering from a mental illness that caused him to lose touch with reality. He was not crazy and could not legally be held in hospital against his will.

He was diagnosed as having a personality disorder, a set of deep-seated problems that impaired his ability to control violent behaviour, deal with everyday issues in a mature way and relate normally to other people. This was not an illness or a chemical imbalance that could be treated with drugs, but a life-long condition that required on-going therapy to improve Jonathan's insight into his problems and help him learn to control them. Jonathan was accepted as an out-patient in the hospital's mental health program, but successful treatment would depend on Jonathan's own motivation, patience and co-operation.

There was no prospect of anyone being able to help Jonathan

unless he wanted to help himself. The first step in therapy would be for Jonathan to accept responsibility for his behaviour and express a sincere desire to change it. But Jonathan had been using drunkenness as an excuse, and by failing to press charges, or tell the police the whole truth, his family had already allowed him to evade legal responsibility for what he had done. He soon began to minimize the significance of his attack on Nancy and even cast doubts as to whether it really took place. On his second visit to the hospital, he told a psychiatrist, "I guess I had too much to drink. They say I hit her. They say I strangled her."

When Jonathan appeared for therapy, he spoke positively about his desire to deal with his problems and change his life. His lack of real commitment was apparent, however, in his attendance, which was described by hospital staff as "sporadic at best." His life was, in fact, still on a downward spiral and this became chillingly apparent on August 14, 1987, when Jonathan attacked Sheila's best friend.

Lindsey, known as Ms J at the inquest, was a slim blonde-haired woman who might have been beautiful if her thin face were not so drawn and pale. She had been friends with Sheila since they were in public school together. She and her ex-husband used to socialize with Jonathan and Sheila during the early years of their respective marriages. Sometimes they would take drugs together. She had always found Jonathan somewhat remote and had never particularly liked him, although she accepted him and trusted him because he was Sheila's husband. After her marriage broke up in 1986, Lindsey stayed with Sheila and Jonathan for six weeks before moving with her two young children into a small house near the Lake Ontario shoreline in the town of Grimsby, about 20 kilometres east of Hamilton.

Lindsey had a housewarming party at the beginning of August 1987. Her next-door neighbour later recalled that she was puzzled by Jonathan's behaviour that night. He spent most of the evening wandering around the outside of the house. He seemed to be pacing in an almost methodical way, as if he were taking measurements.

Two weeks later, Lindsey was alone in the house while her children were with her ex-husband. She was tired after a day's work and went to bed early, sleeping as usual on a couch in her living room. At about 1 a.m. she was awakened by someone banging on the window. It was Jonathan, who urgently told her that he needed help. He looked nervous and he had apparently injured his arm. It did not occur to Lindsey not to let him into the house.

Jonathan paced up and down the house as he told a confusing story about how he had been playing baseball and had been confronted by some men to whom he owned money. He said the men had been chasing him and had followed him up the street. The injury to his arm was just a graze, but he said he was afraid that these men were going to get him. He said that he and Lindsey would have to hide in the house, because the men would recognize his car on the street outside.

Lindsey suggested that he call the police, his mother or Sheila. He rejected her suggestions but he did take the phone, which had a long extension cord, into the kitchen. Lindsey could hear him talking and assumed that he had followed her advice after all.

Without any explanation, however, Jonathan began to go around the house turning lights off. Lindsey followed him, turning the lights back on. Feeling that Jonathan was not making any sense, Lindsey became irritated with him. She decided to ignore him and lie down on the couch, hoping that he would take the hint and leave. While Jonathan loitered in the living room, smoking a cigarette, Lindsey closed her eyes and pretended to fall asleep.

Suddenly she was aware of what sounded like an animal growling, and she felt the blade of a knife sliding down her neck. Jonathan was on the floor behind the couch, growling and holding the knife against her with an outstretched arm. Lindsey screamed and grabbed at the knife. She was able to knock the knife away and she sat up, yelling at Jonathan and pounding him with her fists.

Jonathan seemed stunned for a moment. Lindsey broke free and ran toward the patio door. She had felt safe in her quiet neighbour-hood in the sleepy, small town, so she always left the doors unlocked. But now she realized that the patio door had been locked and bolted. Jonathan must have done that while he wandered around the house. He was on his feet now and chasing her. She ran toward the kitchen door, only to find that it too had been bolted. He was about five feet away from her by the time she managed to get the bolt undone and open the door. She ran to a neighbour's house, screaming hysterically, and pounded on the door. As she ran away, she was aware of Jonathan standing in the doorway of her home and calling out, "Wait a minute."

As her neighbour was trying to calm Lindsey down enough to get a coherent story from her, they heard Jonathan's car race away, spinning its wheels on the gravel road. Since the neighbour had no telephone, they cautiously returned to Lindsey's house. Lindsey's first thought was to call Sheila to warn her that Jonathan was acting like a madman and was probably on his way home. She was amazed at the flat tone with which Sheila responded to her warning. Sheila sighed as if it had all happened before and told her friend that she had better call the police. Lindsey did so and returned to her neigh-bour's house to wait for them.

When two officers arrived about 20 minutes later, Lindsey took them into her house. She noticed at once that the telephone cord had since been cut. A length of severed cord was lying on the floor. Jonathan had returned to the house and his voice could now be heard coming from an upstairs bedroom. He was in the children's room, playing with their toys and talking to himself. Lindsey could hear him pushing her little boy's toy trucks around the floor.

Lindsey bolted from the house and somehow in the confusion Jonathan got out too. He ran past the police down to the lakeshore, where they found him splashing around in the water. According to a police officer's notes, Jonathan gave himself up, saying, "I need help. My mind has gone. I'm all rambling. I put a knife to my friend."

This statement seemed a little pat for a man who had supposedly lost his wits, and the police officer who made the arrest was asked four years later at the inquest if Jonathan had made that statement spontaneously.

"He said it once," replied former constable Raymond Fonger of the Niagara Regional Police, who has since retired after 22 years as a uniformed patrol officer in the force's Grimsby detachment.

Fonger was criticized at the inquest for not collecting any evidence and leaving the cut phone cord and the kitchen knife, which had been used in the assault, lying around at the scene of the crime. But he explained that in his view it was up to the detectives and the "higher ups" in the force to decide whether charges should be laid and whether to conduct an investigation. His priority was to get a man who needed help to the hospital. His view of the situation may have been coloured somewhat by the fact that he thought of the case as a "domestic type thing" and that he thought of the Grimsby beach neighbourhood as a "rough, tough" area, where there was a lot of drinking and drugs. He was also unaware of the fact that Jonathan had driven away from the house and then returned later on foot, presumably to lie in wait for Lindsey, after disconnecting the telephone.

Once Jonathan had been admitted to the St. Catharines General Hospital, Fonger returned to talk to Lindsey. He told her where Jonathan was and that she could go to the police station to lay charges the next day, if she wished. He got the impression that she did not want to. Lindsey did not remember meeting Fonger that night and subsequently maintained that, if she had indicated that she did not want to lay charges, she had been in no state to make such a decision.

Fonger was not expecting that criminal charges would be laid, but in his view they could wait anyway until the man got treatment. He explained, "A mental person gets attention before he goes to jail. That's the way I work, the way I was trained. You can always charge. But you can't always help." But Fonger's training dated from earlier times when matters of this nature were handled more informally, before mental health laws made it difficult for hospitals to detain patients involuntarily and before technical rules of evidence dominated criminal court proceedings.

The sergeant in charge of criminal investigations in Grimsby was well aware that the case would be difficult to prosecute since evidence had not been seized right away. But he had also been given the impression that the victim did not want to press charges and maintained that he was never made aware of important details in the case, such as the cut telephone wire, the fact that Jonathan used a ruse to get into the house or his arrival by car and subsequent return on foot.

In fact, Lindsey found the knife that had been used in the assault on her living room couch the following morning. It had a six-inch serrated blade. She put it aside for the police, but they never asked for it. She brought it to court when she testified at the inquest four years later. It was also Lindsey and her neighbour who found Jonathan's car a few days after the attack, parked about a five-minute walk from the house. Lindsey was chilled by this discovery because it was clear that Jonathan must have been planning to ambush her in her own house, intending as she put it, "to finish what he had started."

According to Lindsey, the police told her that there was no point in laying charges because Jonathan would get treatment at the hospital. However, police officers would later insist that they urged Lindsey to lay charges but found her unwilling to do so. The police maintained that they gave up on the case because they did not have corroborating evidence and they thought the victim would be a reluctant witness. In giving this explanation, police officers glossed over the fact that Jonathan had actually confessed to his crime and that evidence would have been available, if they had bothered to collect it.

But Lindsey had a very good reason to be somewhat confused and ambivalent about laying charges. She had been warned off by Sheila Yeo.

Sheila phoned Lindsey two days after the attack. When she began the conversation, Lindsey was offended that Sheila did not ask her how she was feeling, but only wanted to talk about Jonathan's "poor tormented mind." Lindsey was further affronted when Sheila suggested that she should seek counselling and that it would be good therapy for her to talk to Jonathan. Then Sheila asked Lindsey if she was going to press charges. When Lindsey indicated that she might do so, Sheila warned her that she would get into a lot of trouble if she did. In the past, Lindsey had occasionally supplied Jonathan and Sheila with small quantities of cocaine and hashish. Sheila would tell the police about these transactions if Lindsey pressed charges against Jonathan.

At the inquest, Sheila admitted that this had happened. She acknowledged that it was "a pretty insensitive thing for me to do, a stupid thing to do." She explained that she was worried about her family. She said, "I had two small children. I was really scared about what might happen, scared things might get really messy." Sheila gave another excuse, similar to one that her mother would later use in connection with a third occasion the family tried to cover up for Jonathan. Sheila said that she wanted to talk Lindsey out of laying charges because "I was scared for her about what might happen. I know that victims get revictimized and their credibility comes into question."

Sheila's warning may not have played a large role in ensuring that Jonathan would not be charged. Lindsey maintained that she was not deterred and did try to lay charges. But what Sheila said certainly made her feel betrayed, isolated and insecure. This may well have led Lindsey to give mixed messages to the police, who were perhaps looking for an excuse to drop an investigation that they had already botched.

What Jonathan did changed Lindsey's life. She felt she could no longer trust people. She could no longer work and she was afraid whenever she was alone in her house. She felt somewhat reassured as long as she believed that Jonathan was being held for treatment in a psychiatric institution. That small measure of security was shattered, however, when Lindsey went to a David Bowie concert in Hamilton, just over two weeks after the attack, and saw Jonathan and Sheila. She was angry that he was out on the streets and able to enjoy a concert, while she was still struggling to cope with her feelings of violation and betrayal.

The police officer who put Jonathan in hospital would have shared Lindsey's consternation at seeing him free so soon. When Constable Fonger and his partner chose to seek help for Jonathan, rather than charge him, they made the naive but understandable assumption that he would remain in hospital until he was well. Fonger said, "I'd fear for the safety of anybody if he was to be discharged. You don't hold a knife to a girl's throat one night and never do it again."

Staff at the hospital had a completely different understanding of why police had decided not to charge Jonathan with a criminal offence. For them, it was an indication that the police did not perceive what Jonathan had done to be a serious crime. He did not constitute a genuine threat to public safety in the eyes of the law. In fact, hospital staff had been waiting to find out whether or not Jonathan would be charged before they decided to admit him into the hospital.

It was a general hospital with no secure facilities for dealing with dangerous or criminally insane patients. If serious criminal charges were laid the staff might have considered the possibility that they were dealing with a dangerous psychopath with sexual and sadistic urges. Otherwise, they might easily conclude that someone had over-dramatized a scene involving alcohol and a wife's friend. The chief psychiatrist bluntly explained at the inquest, "If he's a criminal sexual psychopath, I don't want him running around my ward."

Several years later, psychiatrists would, in fact, realize that Jonathan was highly dangerous and had some of the characteristics of what is commonly described as a psychopath. "Psychopath" and "sociopath" are terms for what is now described as an "anti-social personality disorder."

When Jonathan began to minimize the seriousness of the incident involving Lindsey, psychiatrists had no reason to disbelieve him, given that the police had not taken the incident seriously. Jonathan was able to avoid taking responsibility for his actions by pretending that it was all some kind of misunderstanding. He appeared surprised when details like the cut telephone cord or the knife were mentioned to him. One psychiatrist noted that Jonathan was very vague when questioned about details and would say things like, "I don't think I ever threatened her with a knife. She was a friend of mine, a friend of my wife." The psychiatrist commented, "You'd almost have to be a Crown attorney to nail him down." But the Crown attorney had not been involved.

Once again Jonathan had been able to use the mental health system as a way of evading criminal responsibility for his actions. He was again able to deny responsibility and avoid facing his problems in therapy. After two weeks in the hospital as a voluntary patient who could discharge himself at any time, Jonathan was referred for out-patient marriage counselling and an alcohol abuse program.

Jonathan did participate in the alcohol abuse program and went with Sheila to 17 sessions with a marriage counsellor during the following two years. In the meantime, Sheila gave birth to their third child, a boy, in October 1988. It is not possible to say with any confidence that Jonathan did not attack or abuse any other women during that period, but no such incidents came to light. The emphasis in Jonathan's therapy now shifted from his violent behaviour, which he maintained had been greatly exaggerated. He expressed a desire to "move on" to identify and deal with problems in his relationship with Sheila.

At an alcohol abuse clinic, he described the August 13 incident as "very minor" and said it occurred because he was impaired. There was hardly any evidence to show that drinking was a factor in this or other such incidents. His alcohol problems were self-proclaimed and it may be that these too were an excuse for behaviour that would have appeared far more sinister had it occurred while he was sober.

Sheila was well aware of Jonathan's shortcomings in therapy. She told one social worker that her husband "doesn't know the truth, has good intentions, but never follows up, says one thing and does another."

Jonathan never attacked Sheila or his children. He seemed to be in awe of Sheila and very much under her control when he was at home. It was, perhaps, out of a displaced anger toward Sheila that he had attacked her mother and her closest female friend. It is also possible that these attacks were motivated by a more generalized hatred toward women and that the victims were chosen simply because they were close at hand.

Although Jonathan had shown a tendency to attack women who were close to Sheila, she had done little or nothing to warn others. Sheila and her mother not only kept outsiders in the dark about the full extent of Jonathan's problems, but were reluctant to discuss them with other members of the family. Thus, Sheila's 23-year-old cousin, Yvonne, had no idea of the danger to which she was exposing herself as she developed a close, trusting friendship with Jonathan.

Yvonne felt a special bond with Jonathan because she is a Canadian native who had been adopted at an early age into a white family. A shy, loving, somewhat insecure young woman, who was always anxious to please the members of her adoptive family, she often baby-sat for Sheila. She spent a lot of time talking to Jonathan and listening to pop music tapes.

At about 7 a.m. on August 30, 1990, Yvonne was alone in the apartment that she shared with her mother, who had gone to work. She was surprised when Jonathan knocked at the door, but accepted his explanation that he had come to install the fans that Yvonne's mother had just purchased. He came in carrying a large army bag containing some tools. When he opened the bag, he got out some rope and started making knots. He offered to show Yvonne the different kinds of knots he could tie. She was not really interested because she had other plans for the morning, but politely paid attention for a while.

They were sitting in the living room of the apartment. Jonathan asked Yvonne to put out her hand so that he could demonstrate one of his knots. She complied and he tied the rope around her wrist. Yvonne noted that it was a very firm knot, but had no reason to be worried. Jonathan was laughing and she thought he was just fooling around. She let him tie the other wrist, then waited for him to undo the knots. But he just continued to laugh as he pulled them tighter. Yvonne asked him to undo them, but he did not reply. He held the length of rope to which her wrists were bound and started to pull her across the room, through the kitchen, then along the hallway, toward her bedroom.

Yvonne later explained that at this point she still did not know what he was up to. In hindsight, it seemed to her that she had been very naive, but he was her cousin and he was laughing, acting as if he was merely fooling around. She felt scared and, as she put it, "kind of leery," but unsure of what was going on.

There was little that she could do anyway. He was bigger and stronger than her and her wrists were tied tightly together. He threw her onto her bed and, still laughing as if he was thoroughly enjoying himself, he sat on top of her as he tied her wrists and then her ankles to the bed. Yvonne struggled in vain to fight him off and kept asking him to stop, pleading with him to untie her and telling him that the fun was over, that it was getting beyond a joke.

Jonathan continued to laugh as he loosened her clothes, removed his own pants and proceeded to molest and rape her. Yvonne felt paralyzed. She was unable to scream. She was afraid to move, because she thought that might encourage him. He did not say a word and showed no emotion whatsoever, apart from his laughter. When he had finished, he calmly dressed, untied her and got ready to leave, as if nothing had happened.

Yvonne was so shocked that she could no nothing other than follow the routine that she had planned for that morning. She got dressed and went out to a dental appointment. The only way that she could deal with the initial impact of the assault was by acting as if nothing had happened and putting her horror on hold. When she got back from the dentist, she phoned Nancy, her aunt, and asked her to come at once. Yvonne chose to tell Nancy rather than her mother because she was worried that her mother would, as she put, "throw a fit."

It was difficult for Yvonne to say anything and she cried more than she talked, but eventually she managed to tell Nancy what had happened. Responding with concern and efficiency, Nancy took Yvonne to the hospital, where she was examined and introduced to a counsellor from the Sexual Assault Centre. Nancy was present for some of the discussions with the counsellor but tried to distance herself, conscious of the fact that she faced a conflict, since her son-in-law was Yvonne's assailant. The counsellor later assured the coroner's inquest that Nancy did not appear to be trying to persuade her niece not to press charges.

However, the counsellor presented Yvonne with a very bleak picture of the legal system and the way in which victims of sexual assault are treated. She told her that she had to decide within 24 hours whether she wanted the hospital to conduct a demanding and painful examination during which her body would be searched for evidence. She said that once this examination was done, it would be very difficult to prevent police laying charges. The counsellor expressed the opinion that the law often allows rapists to go free and warned Yvonne that she could expect to be questioned aggressively by police and in court.

Yvonne was still in a state of shock when Nancy took her home. There she was confronted with her mother's response, which was as emotional as she had expected. She felt intense pressure to make a decision within 24 hours, because of what the counsellor had told her. Her mother and aunt were not overtly trying to influence her, but she was intensely conscious of the impact that criminal charges would have on Sheila, her children and the rest of the family. She was also afraid that Jonathan might come back and hurt her again. Nancy did not tell her about Jonathan's earlier assaults.

After the three of them had talked for a while, Nancy announced that she was going out to the farm to visit Jonathan and Sheila, because she wanted to "understand what on earth was going on, why this was happening." She asked Yvonne and her mother if they wanted to go with her.

Yvonne decided to go, although she was unsure about it. She was worried that her side of the story would not be told if she was not there. Perhaps Jonathan would convince everyone that the assault did not take place. She would rather have been left alone and been free not to think about it at all. But she felt pressured to make a decision and to explain herself.

While she was still in a state of shock and struggling with her own emotions, Yvonne was being placed in a position where she felt she had to meet her assailant and deal with the complex dynamics of a family in which she desperately wanted to maintain her place. She was afraid, but she recognized that she would have to deal with Sheila and Jonathan sooner or later. She felt that she would be safe, because her aunt and mother would be with her.

Yet, soon after they arrived at the farm, Nancy and her sister went out for a walk, leaving Yvonne alone with the man who had raped her that morning and his wife. Nancy later said that she did not have any concern about doing this, because she trusted Sheila and Jonathan not to hurt Yvonne anymore.

The reason Nancy gave for abandoning her niece in this way was that Sheila was upset with the confrontational tone with which the discussion began. It seemed that Jonathan had admitted to Sheila that something had happened that morning, but implied that it was nothing more than "horsing around." Sheila had the impression that Jonathan and Yvonne had been having some kind of close relationship and that Yvonne was as much to blame for whatever went awry as he was. Sheila was shocked when she heard that Yvonne was tied with a rope. Nancy quickly became angry over the confusion and apparent evasion. She lost her temper and asked, "What on earth is going on here and why is this happening?"

Sheila replied, "Mother, if you're going to yell, I can't deal with anything. I can't understand it myself."

Nancy then asked her sister to go outside with her. She said, "Maybe it would be better if we go for a walk and leave you three to talk about it, because I'm very angry."

Yvonne was apprehensive about being left alone with Jonathan and Sheila, but did not voice any objections. She was feeling confused and extremely anxious, bothered by Jonathan's dishonesty and worried that she would be disbelieved or even blamed. Jonathan was at the same time denying what really happened and offering evasive excuses. He spoke tearfully about the fact that he was adopted and had been the victim of racial prejudice all his life. Yvonne was angered by this and pointed out that she too was adopted and an Indian, but did not go around assaulting people.

At one point, Sheila asked Jonathan to leave and when they were alone asked Yvonne a series of very personal questions. She asked her if she felt dirty after what happened, whether she had taken a shower. Since Sheila later said that she did not believe her cousin's story, it would appear that her motive in asking such intimate details was not so much concern as a desire to probe the truthfulness of Yvonne's account. Sheila asked her bluntly why she was not going to press criminal charges, with the obvious suggestion that it was because her allegation was false. Yvonne replied that it was because she loved her cousins and did not want them hurt or exposed to bad publicity.

When Nancy and her sister returned, they talked about criminal charges and how best to get help for Jonathan. Nancy was convinced that there must be treatment available for him in the community. She worked with prison inmates and everyone in the family was aware of her view that little effective therapy is ever provided in penitentiaries. Sheila assured them that she and Jonathan would seek further help.

Yvonne never received any therapy for her pain and confusion. In all their concern for Jonathan and Sheila, her mother and her aunt apparently neglected to ask Yvonne if she needed help. For years, perhaps for the rest of her life, she would suffer from insecurity and self-doubt because of what Jonathan did. She would also continually wonder if she did the right thing by not pressing charges. She had been alarmed at the prospect of being revictimized by the police and the legal system. It seems not to have occurred to her that the questions they would pose would have been much less probing, insensitive and painful than the questioning from within the family.

Sheila made good on her promise to seek therapy for Jonathan by asking her family doctor to make a referral. She did not tell the doctor the full story. Unless he was seriously interested in changing his ways, there was never much chance that Jonathan would get the kind of treatment that could potentially help him. The doctor's notes recalled that Sheila and Jonathan had spoken only about his "level of anger." They said that he vented this anger by punching inanimate objects, yelling at Sheila and occasionally pushing her. Obviously, this did not seem to concern the physician, who wrote in her notes, "But she is quite a bit bigger than Jonathan."

The doctor was also told that Jonathan did not want to go back to the St. Catharines General Hospital. She would have no reason to suspect that he was afraid to go there again because they knew him too well. She referred him to the Welland County Hospital, a small institution where staff had even less expertise in treating seriously disturbed or violent patients. There Jonathan was assigned a therapist whom he was to see about twice a month. The therapist had been trained in a small, private psychotherapy institute, but was not a medical doctor or a certified psychologist. When he found out, too late, the true extent of Jonathan's problems, he readily admitted that he should not have been treating Jonathan.

Sheila went with Jonathan for the first session. She sat with him as he explained to the therapist that he was having problems with anger, alcohol and self-esteem. Sheila would later claim that she told the therapist about the attacks on her mother, her friend and her cousin, but no such information was recorded in the therapist's notes. In fact, the therapist was left with the impression that the most important issue to be dealt with was Jonathan's "affair" with his cousin and the tensions it had caused in his relationship with Sheila. Initially, Jonathan said he blamed himself for the affair and felt ashamed. But the therapist was working on improving Jonathan's self-esteem and eventually persuaded Jonathan that as two people had been involved he should not blame himself exclusively. The therapist evidently felt that progress was being made.

Jonathan had distanced himself from his crime so thoroughly that he was now able to absolve himself of responsibility. Since Sheila and her family had protected him when he got involved with the law, they may have reinforced in Jonathan the belief that if he promised to seek psychiatric help, he could get away with heinous crimes. In avoiding criminal charges, Jonathan not only escaped the consequences of his actions, but ensured that there was no record of what he had done.

Family members were aware that Jonathan had committed three very serious assaults on people close to him and his wife. With each new assault, it became more apparent that therapy was failing to curb Jonathan's violent and sinister behaviour. Their continued silence ensured that the police, therapists and potential victims would remain ignorant, at least for a while longer, of how dangerous Jonathan could be.

seven

ARMED AND
DANGEROUS

▼

THE NIAGARA ESCARPMENT forms a natural barrier that divides the city of Hamilton in two. Most of the highway accesses that wind their way around its cliffs and up its steep, wooded slopes have no provision for pedestrians, the more hardy of whom have the option of climbing one of several formidable flights of steps. These steps present a challenge, even to the physically fit, and are not well travelled, especially since the surrounding woods are frequented by vagrants, glue-sniffers and under-aged drinkers.

The Wentworth Street steps in the east central section of the city are one of the highest and steepest of these pedestrian accesses, but they offered the quickest route home for a 30-year-old social worker who had been visiting a friend in the downtown area on April 7, 1991. Alison, who was identified as Ms S in the inquest into Jonathan's death, had just moved into an apartment on the escarpment brow. It was a cool evening and she was wearing a heavy sweater over her track suit as she trudged up the metal steps.

As a newcomer to the neighbourhood, Alison was perhaps not fully attuned to its dangers. She was, anyway, strong-willed and not easily intimidated. Although she was a small, slightly built woman, Alison liked to exercise and was determined to keep herself in good shape. She saw no reason why she should not walk up a well-lit, municipally maintained staircase at about 10:30 in the evening.

Even if she was on her guard, the man whom she met on the steps gave her no cause for alarm. He was wearing running shoes, track pants and a T-shirt and was working out vigorously, running up and down a section of the stairway. Alison offered a friendly greeting and a word of encouragement. He seemed like a pleasant, well-spoken man, and they fell into a casual conversation about fitness and training as he walked with her up the steps and along the brow of the escarpment.

It is impossible to say what Jonathan was doing at that time of night on the Wentworth Street steps, miles from his workplace and even further from his home. Perhaps he was just wandering around the city after work, reluctant to go home to Sheila, who was more than eight months pregnant with their fourth child. He was again overwhelmed by the confusion and anger that he felt whenever his wife was expecting a baby.

It may be that he chose the steps as a place where he could work off his intense nervous energy and happened to meet a good-looking woman who was vulnerable and alone. In that case, it was pure coincidence that his car was parked close to her home. But it is also quite likely that Jonathan had been out on the prowl, had spotted Alison earlier, identified her as a potential victim, stalked her and carefully laid his ambush.

He walked with Alison as far as the parking lot of her building, where she said goodbye. She lived in a basement apartment in a somewhat drab, low-rent building. Her job as a counsellor at a social service agency was a responsible one, but not very well paying. Alison had been living with her parents before moving into the apartment, which was still sparsely furnished. She had yet to get curtains, although she had temporarily stuck garbage bags on her bedroom windows.

Soon after she arrived home, Alison heard a knock on the door. She looked through her peephole and saw that it was the jogger whom she had met earlier. She was wary as she had not told him which apartment she lived in. Keeping the door on its chain, she opened it slightly. The man seemed extremely agitated and said he had been assaulted in a nearby park by a group of teenagers. He was holding a pocket knife with a six-inch blade which he said he had taken away from one of the youths. He showed Alison a wound on his right arm, which he said was made by the knife. The skin was broken and it was bleeding slightly.

Alison had doubts about letting him in, but he said that the youths were still after him. He persuaded her to allow him to come inside so that he could call the police and be safe while they waited for the police to come. She let him in and showed him where the phone was. He walked towards it, but did not make a call. Alison assumed that he had decided that he was safe and it was no longer necessary to call for help. She gave him some aloe vera cream for his cut and sat with him at the table while he applied the ointment with a Q-tip.

Jonathan told her that he worked at Dofasco and lived on a pig farm. He said his wife died in childbirth four years earlier and he was still mourning her loss. He also told her that his father was black and his mother was a white British woman with red hair. He told her that he was 32 years old and that his birthday was on September 21. He may have given Alison his real name, although he mumbled when he said it and she later recalled it as Chris Johnson.

Alison was a sensitive and compassionate woman who felt that her visitor wanted to talk about his troubles. She now felt comfortable enough with him to offer him a glass of wine. He talked about how empty his life felt after his wife died and said he had successfully battled a bout of alcohol and drug addiction. He said he found it difficult to meet women. When he described how his wife died in childbirth, Alison noticed that the muscles in his face contorted and he looked off into the distance, in what she took to be very genuine distress.

They talked for just over an hour, during which time Jonathan drank about a glass and a half of wine. Then Alison said that she had to go to work the next morning and it was time for him to leave. When he got up to go, Jonathan said he felt dizzy from the wine, explaining that he was not used to drinking anymore. Alison suggested he call a taxi. Jonathan seemed to think about it for a few moments before deciding to leave on foot.

A few minutes after Jonathan left there was another knock on the door. It was around midnight and Alison was feeling very tired as she cleared the glasses from the table and threw away the Q-tip. Alison looked through the peephole and saw that it was Jonathan. Assuming that he had changed his mind about calling a taxi, she pulled the door open and turned away to walk toward the phone. She wondered which taxi company he would like her to call and turned toward him as she started to ask the question.

Jonathan was standing inside the door holding a rifle. He was just a few feet away from Alison, but he had the rifle mounted on his shoulder and was looking at her through the sight, his finger poised on the trigger. It was an old gun, made of scratched, dull metal and worn, dark wood, but nonetheless menacing. Alison's description of the weapon matched that of the gun which Jonathan subsequently used in two murders. It is not known how Jonathan obtained this rifle or where it came from.

Speaking in an aggressive, authoritative tone that had been completely absent in his earlier conversation, Jonathan told Alison to go into the bathroom. Alison responded with disbelief and instinctive courage as she took a few steps toward him, saying, "I don't understand, Chris. What are you doing?"

Jonathan made an impatient motion with the barrel of his gun and said, "Go to the bathroom. I don't want anybody to see what I'm going to do to you."

Alison obeyed and he followed her into the bathroom, shutting the door behind them. Jonathan put the rifle down and said, "I'm really upset. You wouldn't believe how upset I am. I need a hug."

As Alison complied with this demand, she took stock of the fact that Jonathan was bigger and stronger than her, muscular and evidently physically fit enough to have put himself through a vigorous workout. She looked at the rifle which he had propped against the wall tantalizingly within her reach, but she had never even touched a gun in her life and had no confidence in her ability to use it, even if she were able to wrest it away from him.

Alison felt that her best chance of survival did not lie in some bold gesture or desperate struggle, but in keeping her wits about her. This was going to require a more patient form of courage. In an effort to get him talking and gain some insight, she asked him where he got the gun and he told her that he found it outside the apartment. He said he wasn't even sure that it worked. Then he brazenly contradicted his first statement by saying that he had not fired it for a long time. From his pocket, he produced a package of ammunition. He seemed to be showing off as he insisted that Alison touch one of the long, thin, sharply pointed copper shells. She was not sure whether she touched it or not, as her hands were stiff with terror and her senses felt numbed.

Jonathan told Alison that he did not want to hurt her, but he felt like killing himself. Alison began talking to Jonathan as she would to a client at the social agency where she worked. Her professional skills, which she applied during the next few hours, may well have saved her life. She asked him if there was anybody he could phone and talk to. She suggested his mother or his drug and alcohol addiction counsellor.

When he rejected this suggestion, Alison tried to persuade him that he would feel more comfortable sitting at the dining room table and talking there. She said she felt cramped in the bathroom. But Jonathan said he did not want to do that as the neighbours would see in. Then Alison told him that she felt thirsty and needed a drink. She was surprised to find that he did go out to the kitchen to get her a glass, but he did not go far enough away to give her a realistic chance of escaping. Even if he did not shoot her, he would have been able to catch her before she reached the telephone or the front door.

His manner continually alternated between two extremes. At one moment, he seemed to be aware of what he was doing, apologetic, even considerate to a degree, promising Alison that he would not hurt her, but never for a moment letting down his guard or relinquishing control. Then he seemed to disconnect from reality, becoming cold and aggressive. It was at these moments that he also appeared most dangerous and volatile.

Alison found that if she reasoned with Jonathan she could usually pull him back from his more dangerous state. She tried to keep him calm and she avoided doing anything that he might interpret as being aggressive. He had told her that he had never set out to hurt anybody, but in the past several people had hurt him first and then he had hurt them really badly. At one point, when Jonathan was in his more sympathetic mode, Alison almost persuaded him that they should go outside for some fresh air. She told him that he was obviously upset and just needed to talk about it. She suggested that they walk down to the doughnut shop for a coffee. She actually had her hand on the handle of the apartment door when Jonathan raised his gun to her head and ordered her back into the bathroom.

Jonathan told her, "When I look in the mirror I see two of me physically, two images." He said he had told his counsellor in Welland about this and the counsellor told him that there was a war going on inside him between his good and bad sides. But Jonathan said that there were actually three sides he could identify: the good, the bad and the animal. He told Alison that he was trying to keep the animal side under control because he did not want to hurt her. At one point, he poured water down the inside of his pants, explaining that he was trying not to get hard.

So far, Alison had been able to use her wits to dissuade

Jonathan from molesting her sexually. They had been in the bath-room for about an hour when Jonathan noticed that the windows in the bedroom were completely covered so that no one would be able to see in from the outside. He told Alison to go into the bed-room. He took out the knife that he had shown her earlier and held it to her throat. Then he closed his eyes and ordered her to take her clothes off. She tried to prevaricate, but he merely repeated his order and pressed the point of the knife against her.

For the next several hours, Jonathan alternately molested Alison and pulled back apologetically, allowing her to lie terrified on the bed and await his next assault. He always stopped short of actual penetration and did not seem to be trying to inflict physical pain. Perhaps that is what he meant by his continual protestation that he was not going to hurt her.

Obviously this attack had far less to do with sexual desire than with a lust for power, control and domination. The same can be said for most sexual assaults, but in this case the violence mostly took the form of extreme menace, which persisted over several hours. It was a slow torture in which Alison was continually being exposed to gross indignities and prolonged psychological terror. All the while, she felt that in order to stay alive she had to concentrate very hard on appearing calm, reasonable and even sympathetic.

On a couple of occasions, Jonathan allowed Alison to go to the bathroom. The first time he followed her, carrying his gun, and then demonstrated what seemed like an absurd streak of prudery for someone perpetrating a sexual assault by turning his back on her while she used the toilet. When he later let her go to the bathroom again, he did not follow her and she thought for a moment that she might have an opportunity to escape. But he was lurking in a door-way and grabbed her as she walked across the room.

Sometimes, while Alison tried to reason with Jonathan, he sat on the bed and talked. He would sit holding the knife, waving it around and running the blade up and down on his chest and his arms. He told her that he knew that what he was doing was bad, but he felt empowered. At one point, he confided, "I'm trying to figure out what I'm going to do about this mess I'm into."

"What do you mean?" Alison asked.

"Do you realize that you could charge me with forcible confinement right now?" he replied.

Alison pretended that she did not know that and would never consider doing such a thing. She prayed that he would believe her.

A little later, Jonathan got up to go to the washroom and Alison relaxed for a moment while he was gone. She did not hear him return to the room, but, when she looked up, she saw him standing naked at the end of the bed, holding the rifle against his shoulder and looking through the sights as he aimed the barrel at her from about four feet away. He said, "I'm going to kill you." Alison waited as he stood silent and motionless for a few moments before putting the gun down and lying down again on the bed.

This was perhaps the first time in his career of escalating violence that Jonathan had threatened to kill one of his victims. Although he had used knives and attempted to strangle women in his earlier attacks, he had soon desisted or allowed them to escape. He carried out his attack on his cousin Yvonne with unwavering brutality, but without threatening her life. Now Jonathan was armed with a gun and he was attacking a stranger, rather than a family member or friend. His behaviour had become more dangerous, more bizarre and even less under control.

Alison was sure that she was going to die, unless she could somehow convince him that she would not call the police when he left. He had made it clear to her that he would kill rather than leave a witness who would testify against him. She repeatedly told him that she felt sympathy for him and realized he had problems. She assured him that she wasn't interested in calling the police because there was too much hassle involved. She said that all she wanted was that he should leave her now so she could get some sleep and be able to get to work in the morning. Jonathan offered to give her a ride to work and Alison said that would be great, that she would really appreciate it.

It might seem incredible that Jonathan should have been convinced by Alison. But all his experience so far had shown him that women were afraid to call the police or else could not get the police to take their stories seriously. Perhaps he believed that he had once again convinced a victim that he was a troubled soul who needed help and sympathy. Also, because he had no concept whatsoever of healthy consensual sex, he may very well have persuaded himself that what he had done was not too bad. He may even have deluded himself into believing that Alison had some good feelings for him. After all, his cousin, his mother-in-law and Sheila had all continued to love him, in spite of what he had done.

Jonathan told Alison that he had to go out for a little while and that he would come back with his car to give her a ride to work. He asked for a blanket under which he could conceal his rifle, as it was now becoming light outside. He did, in fact, return about 15 minutes later and seemed surprised to find that Alison had locked the door and was refusing to let him in. She shouted to him through the window that she was getting ready for work and did not want to let him in. He told her that he was not sure that he would be able to come back to give her a ride to work and that he had left her blanket by the front door.

Alison was almost paralyzed with shock. For six hours she had been terrorized and subjected to gross indignities. After fighting a psychological battle for her life, she felt drained of all energy or feeling, disconnected from both her inner self and the outside world. She was afraid to go out, afraid to stay in her apartment. For a while, she did nothing.

▼

It might seem obvious that she should immediately have called the police, but that is not the perspective of someone who has gone through such an ordeal. Like other victims in similar circumstances, Alison felt too fragile at first to talk to strangers. She was afraid of encountering another cold and authoritarian male voice. She phoned her work to leave a message that she would not be coming in. She talked to her martial arts instructor and then a male friend. Her friend urged her to call the police and she finally did so, more than an hour-and-a-half after Jonathan had left.

Constable Kenneth Wilson, who was sent to her apartment at 7:40 a.m., was suspicious of the fact that Alison had waited so long before calling police. He had been a police officer for 15 years and should have known that it is common for victims to wait that long and indeed far longer. But he was a beat constable with no expertise in dealing with sexual assault cases. He did accept Alison's explanation that she had delayed reporting the attack because she was afraid that her assailant might retaliate. But from the very beginning, he was inclined to treat Alison's story with scepticism.

It seemed strange to Constable Wilson that this woman was behaving so calmly. He would have expected someone who had gone through the kind of ordeal that she described to be sobbing and acting hysterically. It did not occur to him that Alison had been forced to stay calm for six hours in order to save her life and had not returned to a normal state. He did not realize that different people respond to trauma in different ways. If he had been given more training in dealing with victims of sexual assault, he would have realized that the most dreadful ordeals sometimes leave victims emotionally numbed for hours or even days, just as the body is often numb to physical pain in cases of severe injury.

The initial police response to Alison's complaint would later be described as a lesson in how not to deal with a sexual assault victim. It was, in fact, largely as a result of the way in which this case was handled that the Hamilton-Wentworth police subsequently followed the lead of other jurisdictions in setting up a special sexual assault team which would be trained to show sensitivity to victims and understand their special needs. The way in which Constable Wilson treated Alison tended to confirm the widespread belief that sexual assault victims are re-victimized by the law. It demonstrated very clearly that some of Jonathan's earlier victims had good reason to be afraid to tell their story to police.

Wilson noted that Alison had sustained no injuries in the assault. The only evidence that she could suggest to prove that the man had been in her apartment was his wine glass and the Q-tip that he used to dress his wound. Wilson said that she should put the glass aside so that it could be examined later for fingerprints and he asked to see the Q-tip. He could not see any blood on it. Wilson felt this may be evidence that Alison's story was false. He apparently failed to consider the possibility that the assailant's wound had been very superficial and was no longer bleeding when Alison applied the swab. Although police officers are trained to keep their feelings to themselves while conducting an investigation, Wilson could not help allowing a note of skepticism to enter his voice.

"I shouldn't have called the police," said Alison, as she realized that the officer did not believe her story.

Wilson tried to reassure her by saying that it did not matter whether he believed her or not because the allegation would be investigated by detectives anyway. He asked her to keep the Q-tip, because, as he noted later, he believed that the detectives would be interested in it one way or another.

He had been looking around the apartment and noticed that it was very sparsely furnished. Alison had given him her parents' address and they lived in an affluent neighbourhood. Constable Wilson began to wonder why Alison was living in a basement apartment. He thought perhaps she might have some problems. She seemed to be reluctant to answer questions about her family. It never crossed Wilson's mind that the reason for that may have been that she did not want her family to know anything about her ordeal. It did occur to him, however, that the Hamilton Psychiatric Hospital was also located on the escarpment brow less than two miles away. He knew that many ex-psychiatric patients lived in low-rent apartments. He made a mental note that he should make some further inquiries.

Wilson felt that there was something bizarre about Alison's story. He explained at the inquest into Jonathan's death, "I think anybody should be able to walk anywhere they want in the city, but the Wentworth Street steps at 11 o'clock are not a prudent place for a female to be alone. The contact was made there. That's where you expect that kind of man to be hanging out. She walked with the man, a total stranger, and didn't take precaution as to whether she was being followed. This seemed to be very imprudent or naive on her part. It didn't seem quite right to me or normal. The guy follows her back and half-an-hour later he's knocking on her door. Bells don't go off and she lets the guy in. It wasn't normal behaviour. At this point I thought I should check her out."

The police officer told Alison that another officer would come to talk to her shortly and pick up the wine glass for fingerprinting. As he left, Alison believed that he told her, "I'm going to check you out." Wilson later denied making such a comment, although, later at the inquest, he used the same words in describing what he had been thinking. He explained that it would have been a very bad career move for him to say something like that and to act like "a jerk" to a sexual assault complainant.

Alison assumed that the other officer would be arriving within an hour or two and lay down on her bed to wait for him and for her friend Mike, who had told her when she phoned him that morning that he would come to see her. Soon after Mike arrived, there was a knock on the door. Alison looked through the peephole and saw Jonathan. She screamed and ran into her bedroom. Mike, who was a burly young man, suggested that he grab the assailant and hold him while Alison called the police. But Alison was in hysterics and said that she just wanted Mike to get rid of him.

Jonathan knocked more loudly on the door and shouted, "Alison, I know you're in there." He tried to look in through the peephole and Mike, who was looking out, saw his eye pressed up against the door. Jonathan then stepped back, shouted the same thing again, and started pacing very briskly up and down in front of the door, holding his hands up to his head and pressing his fingers against his temples.

Mike called out to him, "I'm Alison's boyfriend. I want you to leave."

Jonathan went to a window and tried again to get Alison's attention. Mike opened the window a crack and Jonathan asked him where Alison was. Mike asked Jonathan if he had been there the night before. Jonathan replied that he had and said that he wanted to apologize. Mike was amazed that this man would have the nerve to stand there talking to him after what had happened. Jonathan said, "Tell Alison I'm really sorry. It will never happen again."

Mike replied, "No, it won't. I live with her. I'm her boyfriend. I was out working last night, but I'll be here next time. The police will be looking for you and they'll want to talk to you anyways. You'd better turn yourself in."

Jonathan replied that he had already talked to the police and explained to them what happened. He said it was "all straightened out." He again asked Mike to tell Alison that he would not be back and that it would never happen ever again.

Mike decided to apprehend him, even though Alison had told him not to. He ran outside, heedless of the danger that the man might still have a weapon. It did not make sense to him that this man should be allowed to go free. But when Mike got to the front of the building a few moments later, the man was nowhere in sight. Mike searched all the hiding places he could think of and looked in all directions, but Jonathan had disappeared.

Alison was now beside herself with fear. She lay curled up on her bed and Mike watched over her while they waited for the arrival of the other police officer whom Constable Wilson had promised to send. But no one came.

Meanwhile, Wilson was following up on Alison's allegations in his own way. He had already made the decision that this was not a serious crime. A serious crime would have required that detectives and identification officers be called immediately to search the scene for evidence, interview the complainant while events were still fresh in her mind and provide her with protection, since her assailant was still at large and had threatened to return. Wilson knew that the identification officers were usually very busy early in the morning and did not want to disturb them. He had heard about several false allegations of sexual assault which had caused detectives to waste a lot of time, and he felt that he could save investigators some trouble by evaluating the truthfulness of this woman's story himself.

As soon as he got back to the police station, the constable did a record search to see if Alison's name had come up in connection with any previous investigation. He was looking to see if she had made false reports in the past and if there was any evidence to suggest that she suffered from alcoholism or mental illness. On finding no such information, he decided to call her parents' home. He did not consider the fact that a sexual assault complainant is usually accorded privacy and that Alison may not have wanted her family to know. Wilson assumed that family members would be the first people that any "normal" person would turn to in such circumstances.

He called Alison's brother, told him that his sister had made a complaint to police and asked him if she had ever "done time in a mental home." Mystified by the question, her brother replied that Alison had not ever had any psychiatric problems, but that they had another brother who was a schizophrenic.

After receiving this information, Constable Wilson went to see Brian Leng, the detective on duty, and gave a verbal report. He said that he had received a sexual assault complaint, but did not believe the woman's story. He added that he had called a family member and found out that she had a brother who was schizophrenic. Since the officer seemed to have grounds to believe that this was a frivolous complaint, the detective got on with other pressing business and assumed that he would receive a written report on this matter at some later time.

Mike stayed with Alison until late that night, as they waited in vain for the police to return. He tried to reassure her by telling her he was convinced that he had scared the man off and that he would not come back. He urged Alison to stay at his house, but Alison replied, "I'm not going to be tormented and scared out of my own apartment. If I let that happen, what's going to happen to me?" Alison insisted on spending the night alone, but she was too terrified to sleep.

Detective Leng did not receive Constable Wilson's written report until the next day, when he arrived for an evening shift at 6 p.m. After a brief account of Alison's allegations, Wilson added his own comments: "Writer is obviously sceptical about this story. No HWRP (Hamilton-Wentworth Regional Police) occurrences on file for woman. I spoke to 23-year-old brother who confirms her lack of mental history, although another brother is schizophrenic. She booked off sick today as a result of last night's 'incident' — her behaviour caused me to wonder about her. Writer tried not to show too much of a sceptical attitude, but, after she was unable to produce any evidence, she knew that her story was not credible."

It did not seem like a case to be given high priority and Leng found himself busy with other investigations. He finally went to see Alison at about 9:30 p.m. that evening, April 8, collected the wine glass and bottle and arranged for her to go to the police station a few days later to make a statement. By this time, Alison was extremely frustrated with the police and not inclined to be as co-operative as she might have been at first.

Alison was tired on the night that she was supposed to give her statement. Leng sensed this, after he had talked to her for a little while, and suggested that she go home and write her statement out on her own computer. She readily agreed to do this, especially as she was getting impatient with the speed at which Leng, a two-finger typist, was recording her information. She was relieved to find that the detective treated her in a more courteous and professional manner, showing concern and not exhibiting any scepticism about her story.

Leng was one of six detectives working at the Hamilton Mountain police station. He and his colleagues had a heavy caseload and handled all crimes in their district. There was no system in place for giving priority to certain types of crimes, so that Leng found himself continually interrupting ongoing investigations in order to handle immediate situations. If a housebreaker was arrested and brought into the police station for processing, Leng or one of the other detectives had to make sure that the accused was interviewed properly and accorded his rights to legal representation. This meant that they often had to drop important investigative work on more serious crimes.

The assault on Alison was just one of many ongoing cases that Leng had to deal with. Later, Leng insisted that he treated it as seriously as any other case on the books. But it is difficult to believe that he had not been influenced by the doubts that Constable Wilson had raised.

Nevertheless, Leng did follow up on the few leads that he had, checking pig farms in the Smithville area, asking the Dofasco personnel office if they had an employee named Chris Johnson and showing Alison and her friend photographs of known sex offenders. A fingerprint was found on the wine glass and a copy of it was sent to the Royal Canadian Mounted Police in Ottawa, where a record was kept of the fingerprints of all people charged with criminal offences in Canada.

On May 1, three weeks after the assault, the print on the glass was matched with a fingerprint of Jonathan Yeo, which was taken when he was charged in connection with the starter's pistol six years earlier. When Leng checked police records, he found that Jonathan's date of birth was the same as that which Alison had been told by her assailant. The case now took on a more serious complexion.

Still Leng was in no hurry to make an arrest. He was concerned that he did not yet have a statement from Alison. The statement should have been taken immediately after the assault and now its absence left a hole in the case against Jonathan. There was some question in the investigator's mind as to whether the only witness was willing to come forward with her evidence.

Until Leng saw her statement, he did not have a complete picture of what was alleged to have happened. Apart from the disturbing allegations Alison had made, the police had no information to suggest that Jonathan was a dangerous man who should be arrested as quickly as possible. No record was found to suggest that he had been involved in any offence other than a relatively minor weapons conviction six years before. Somewhere in the Hamilton police files, there was a microfiche of a report on the 1984 incident when he broke into the lobby of Janet's house. Similarly, there would have been a record somewhere of the fact that Jonathan was taken in for psychiatric examination after the 1987 incident at Nancy's apartment, which had been described to police as a suicidal gesture.

Leng was not aware of either of these records, nor were they easily available. The attack on Sheila's friend in 1987 had been investigated by the Niagara Regional Police and their reports were not easy to access by the Hamilton-Wentworth Regional Police. In fact, the Niagara force had a policy of destroying its occurrence reports after three years.

Alison was angry with the way in which the police had treated her. She also found it difficult to write her statement, because it meant remembering details that she would rather put out of her mind. On May 10, she finally agreed to let Leng interview her and type a statement for her to sign. After the interview, Leng told her that he was going to arrest Jonathan and charge him with unlawful confinement, sexual assault with a weapon and threatening death.

Although Detective Leng had decided to arrest Jonathan, he put it off for a few days because he was busy with other tasks. He apparently still failed to see what a serious criminal he was dealing with. He did not seem to have the whole picture in his mind, partly because of the length of time that the investigation had taken and the way that it had been sandwiched between other investigations. Consequently, as he prepared to make his arrest, Leng made a crucial mistake. He failed to look for Jonathan's gun.

A year later, at the inquest into Jonathan's death, Leng acknowledged that this was an oversight. He offered small comfort to Priscilla de Villiers when he promised that he would not make the same mistake again: "Hindsight is twenty-twenty. Obviously, if I had a similar case, I'd take a closer look. I'd be a fool not to. We all learn from our experiences."

Jonathan's house was out in the country and in another jurisdiction. Leng would have to do some further investigation to find out when Jonathan would be home. Then he would have had to consult the Niagara Regional Police and arrange for one of their officers to accompany him, as well as organize transportation back to Hamilton. Leng felt that he was too busy to do any of these things and that it would be a lot easier to simply pick up the phone and ask Jonathan to come to the police station voluntarily.

On May 13, Leng dialled Jonathan's number and asked to speak to Chris. Jonathan came to the phone and the detective told him that he wanted to speak to Chris Yeo about a criminal offence. Leng knew that Jonathan's full name was Jonathan Christopher Yeo, but addressed him as Chris, since that was the name that Jonathan had given Alison. An innocent person would probably have explained that he did not go by that name, but Jonathan simply replied, "I'll try and get down."

Until then, Jonathan believed that he had managed to get away scot-free. He was in good spirits when he saw his therapist on May 8. He talked enthusiastically about the work that he was going to do to improve his home. A month earlier, the therapist — who had no idea what was really going on in Jonathan's life — had noted that his patient seemed to be falling apart. Jonathan told him, three days after the assault on Alison, "I want to be in the dark, stay in the dark. I can't face my life." Jonathan described himself as empty, lost, machine-like, devoid of any sense of who he was.

When the Yeos' fourth baby was born on April 24, Sheila's mother, Nancy, arrived at the hospital for a visit only to find Jonathan sitting by himself holding the baby. She asked him where Sheila was and he responded with a stricken look. He told her that the delivery had not gone well. She asked again about Sheila but he merely repeated himself and added that Sheila had had a very hard time. There had in fact been no problems with the delivery and Jonathan was perhaps indulging the fantasy that he had communicated to Alison about his wife dying in childbirth. However, when he next saw his therapist, he said that he was very excited about his daughter's birth, that it had brought him and Sheila closer together and lifted him out of his feelings of hopelessness and depression.

Even after Leng's phone call on May 13, Jonathan probably felt confident that he could talk his way out of trouble on this occasion, as he had in the past. The fact that the detective asked him to appear voluntarily at the police station seemed to indicate that the allegation was not being taken too seriously. It also gave Jonathan an opportunity to present himself to the police in a favourable light.

A few hours later, Jonathan arrived at the station with Sheila and Nancy's friend, the minister. It is not often that a man accused of a violent sexual assault can demonstrate that he has the support of his wife and a representative of the church. This obviously impressed Leng, who later commented, "Obviously he wasn't someone from off the street. Somebody who did go to church in today's society shows some responsibility." Leng was also made aware that Jonathan was a working man with four children to support. These were factors in Jonathan's favour when he later applied for release on bail.

Now, it would be up to a court, and not the police, to decide whether Jonathan should be allowed to go free while awaiting his trial. But Leng would make his recommendation to the Crown attorney and in his mind Jonathan was a suitable candidate for bail. Accused people have a right to bail under the law, unless it can be proven that they are likely not to show up in court for their trial or would present a threat to public safety if released. Jonathan had given himself up voluntarily. He was a homeowner, with a good job and a family, all of which suggested that his roots in the community were solid enough that he was unlikely to run. Leng did not feel that he had any information that suggested that Jonathan was a danger to other people.

Leng interviewed Jonathan alone and asked him if he had any health problems. Jonathan mentioned that he was receiving counselling for mental health problems, but Leng did not follow this up by seeking any further information. It was later suggested that the investigator should have made more effort to find out about Jonathan's psychiatric history. But Leng explained that mental health is not an area in which police have any training or expertise. He would not have known where to start and he already had several hours of paper work to complete. As it was, it would be 3 a.m. before Leng had finished typing all the reports that he was required to prepare before the bail hearing.

Police are limited by law as to what they can ask without offering a suspect the right to have a lawyer present. Leng informed

Jonathan of this right, told him he was under arrest and gave him a brief account of the allegations against him. Jonathan showed no emotion and said that he did not know Alison. This statement would have been useful for the prosecution if the case had come to trial, since the fingerprint on the wine glass would prove that Jonathan was lying. It would make it difficult for him to claim that he had visited Alison that night but that nothing had happened. Leng did not have an opportunity to obtain any further information from Jonathan, as Jonathan effectively terminated the interview by asking to see a lawyer.

James Child, an experienced defence lawyer, was called and given an opportunity to talk to Jonathan. Before seeing the lawyer Jonathan had been calm, though he had seemed understandably tense. Afterwards, Leng observed that the side of Jonathan's face was shaking violently as he clenched his jaw with his fist. After talking to Child, Jonathan realized, for the first time, what serious trouble he was in.

eight

RELEASING
A TIME BOMB

▼

JONATHAN PANICKED WHEN HE WAS PLACED IN JAIL. He spoke of killing himself and would wake up crying, overwhelmed with shame, embarrassment and anxiety. A psychiatrist in the Hamilton-Wentworth Detention Centre prescribed anti-depressants and placed him on a suicide watch, which involved the added indignity of wearing a fire resistant "baby doll" gown. It was probably during the three-and-a-half weeks that he was waiting in jail for his bail hearing that Jonathan formed the resolve that he would never allow himself to be taken captive again, even if it meant killing himself or others. Jonathan told his brother, James, when he visited, "I can't be caged."

At first, Jonathan was under the impression that he would be released on bail within a few days of his arrest. But his lawyer had the case adjourned, because he wanted to get an opinion from a psychiatrist. Jonathan was claiming that he could not remember what happened on the night of the alleged assault and it appeared that psychiatric evidence might provide the best line of defence.

A psychiatrist, hired by defence lawyer James Child, interviewed Jonathan and came to the conclusion that he was not mentally ill, but that he could present a danger to society. Accepting Jonathan's story that he had been drinking heavily before the attack on Alison, the psychiatrist believed that it was possible that he suffered from amnesia due to an alcoholic blackout. The psychiatrist formed the opinion that Jonathan would remain potentially violent against others and himself if he continued to drink or use drugs.

The psychiatrist sent the lawyer a confidential report of his findings, but did not ever expect it to see the light of day. In the eyes of the law, a report commissioned by a defence lawyer is regarded as being as private as the conversations between a lawyer and a client. It will never be disclosed, unless it is helpful to the defence. Clearly, this was not the kind of evidence that the defence would want to present at a bail hearing, since it suggested that Jonathan would present a risk to the public if he were released.

The report did, however, suggest an avenue for a possible defence at a subsequent trial. The court would probably deal more leniently with Jonathan if it were found that he committed his crimes while in an alcoholic haze, especially if he was able to tell the judge that he had enrolled in a treatment program. The lawyer therefore consulted Jonathan's family doctor about the possibility of getting him a full psychiatric assessment. This would perhaps provide evidence of his problem and could lead to a treatment program. An arrangement was made for Jonathan to go for a four-week assessment at the Clarke Institute of Psychiatry in Toronto, one of Canada's most prestigious psychiatric institutions. But he could not avail himself of this opportunity as long as he was being held in custody. In order to get this assessment, he would have to be released on bail.

Child did not anticipate that this would be difficult. All people charged with criminal offences are considered innocent until proven guilty. They have a right to their liberty, unless it can be proven that it would not be in the interests of justice to release them. The law requires that they must be released from custody, unless it can be proved either that they are not likely to show up for their trial voluntarily or that they would be a threat to public safety if they were at large. For an accused person to be held in jail before his or her trial is the exception rather than the rule.

In most cases, suspects are routinely released on their own undertaking that they will appear in court for trial. In more serious cases, the court may set bail, a sum to be posted with the court, which would be forfeited if the accused person failed to appear for trial. The court may also stipulate certain conditions which the accused must agree to follow.

In the majority of cases, lawyers representing the Crown and defence reach an agreement about the conditions of release and the amount of bail. This agreement is then routinely approved in a court presided over by a justice of the peace, a court official appointed by the provincial government who does not necessarily have any legal training or background.

If the Crown and defence cannot agree, a bail hearing will be conducted. These are also generally presided over by justices of the peace and the rules of evidence are much looser than would be expected in a criminal trial. A police officer or the Crown lawyer briefly tells the justice the salient details of the case, after which the Crown and defence may call evidence about the background of the accused and the terms of the proposed bail. Both parties make brief submissions and the justice usually makes an immediate decision.

In 1991, bail cases in Hamilton were considered in the chaotic environment of an overcrowded court house, which lawyers, judges and police officers alike described as "a zoo." There were plans afoot to replace the converted office buildings which housed the Ontario Court's Provincial Division because its woefully inadequate facilities were unable to cope with its huge volume of cases. The Provincial Division was the lowest level of the criminal justice system to which all cases were originally assigned. It dealt with everything from shoplifting to preliminary hearings in murder cases, which would eventually be heard in the more sedate setting of a higher court. The lobbies and corridors of the Provincial Division courts were almost always packed. Accused people milled around waiting to be called into the crowded courtrooms and lawyers searched for clients or witnesses, whom they were forced to interview in these bustling public areas because there was no office space available.

Jonathan was one of 188 people due to appear in Number One Court on Friday, June 7, 1991. Of these, 162 were there simply to be remanded to another date, but 26 required some decision as to bail. Michael Fox, the young assistant Crown attorney who was assigned to the court that day, received the list of names and a cartload of related documents just half-an-hour before the court was due to open. This was the accepted routine at the time — later to be revised in light of the mistakes that were made in handling Jonathan's case.

Fox, who had graduated from law school just two years earlier, was not yet accustomed to speed-reading more than two dozen case files, making decisions about how to handle each of them, entering into negotiations with lawyers and planning strategies for court hearings — all in the space of half-an-hour or less. The senior Crown attorney claimed that it could be done in that time and the system was designed with the expectation that it would be done. Fox found it impossible to read all the documents.

Under the circumstances, it would have been easy for Fox to have gone along with the investigating police officer's recommendation in Jonathan's case: to release Jonathan on bail, subject to certain conditions. But Fox read enough of the file to see that this was a very serious crime and decided to oppose bail. The defence lawyer tried to change Fox's mind when they met in the corridor outside the court. Child told Fox that his client was an alcoholic who became violent when drunk and had been trying for a long time to get treatment for his problems. Child said he had arranged for Jonathan to go for psychiatric assessment at the Clarke Institute and he would be kept there if it was found that he was dangerous. He suggested that it would be appropriate to agree to Jonathan being released on bail that would be posted by his wife on condition that he did not drink.

Fox refused to agree to this, taking the position that Jonathan could get treatment, if he wanted it, in custody. The assistant Crown attorney was now perplexed because the defence lawyer had told him outside the courtroom that he had psychiatric information suggesting that his client was sometimes violent, but was obviously not planning to share that information with the court. Fox could not give evidence on his own about something that he had learned in conversation with the defence lawyer. He had to try to find another way of getting the information introduced into evidence.

Fox had the case adjourned until the afternoon and used his lunch hour to seek advice from more experienced prosecutors. They suggested that the best tactic would be to wait until the accused man's wife was called to the witness stand to testify about bail and then cross-examine her about her husband's drinking habits and psychiatric problems. This was the strategy on which Fox based his case. He did not realize that the files he had not read contained a statement recording Alison's account of bizarre comments and behaviour that would have provided compelling evidence about Jonathan's dangerous mental state. Had he been a more experienced prosecutor, Fox might have asked for time to review his file. But he was a young man trying to prove himself before a justice of the peace who apparently expected cases to be presented expeditiously.

A transcript of the hearing was just 14 pages long and many people who subsequently listened to a tape recording of the proceedings were shocked by the hasty, off-handed manner in which the court resolved what later proved to be a matter of life and death.

A police officer read a brief description of the allegations that had been prepared by Detective Leng. The officer misread one portion, omitting to say that Jonathan had a gun when he returned to the apartment. But there was another reference to the gun later in the narrative, so Fox did not think it was necessary to draw the court's attention to the earlier oversight. Some of the details the officer read were new to Fox. Fox felt that the justice of the peace would have been able to see from what the officer said that this was a serious offence and that the Crown had a strong case. He did not want to strain the justice's patience by trying to underline these facts for her with further questions or submissions.

Sheila was called by the defence and gave details of Jonathan's job, their children and their property, which she estimated as being worth about $200,000. Fox then tried to elicit the information that he was seeking by asking her, "Does he drink?" He was completely taken aback when Sheila replied, "Not that I know of." Fox asked more questions, but felt he was getting nothing but evasive answers. When he asked Sheila if she had ever seen a gun in the house, she said she had not. She was reminded of the starter's pistol in 1984 and said there were no guns in her house now.

Perhaps it was partly youth and inexperience that led Fox to assume that everyone in the courtroom, including the justice of the peace, shared his belief that Sheila was not a credible witness. He even said he doubted whether Sheila was really Jonathan's wife. Fox could not comprehend how or why a woman would go to the extent of giving evasive answers under oath in order to protect a husband who had terrorized and sexually assaulted another woman. Fox decided that there was no point in questioning Sheila any further, since he was sure that she must have made a bad impression on the court.

The defence lawyer made a very brief submission. He said that this was an isolated incident with only one witness. Since Jonathan had strong roots in the community and there was no indication that he was a danger to the public, he should be released, the lawyer argued. He was able to make this submission because the court had not heard any evidence about psychiatric assessment which suggested that Jonathan was violent when drunk.

Fox's submissions were similarly short and covered just ten lines

in the transcript. He admitted that the offence was a solitary incident, but pointed out that there had been a previous weapons conviction. He said he did not think that Sheila was credible and was
not a suitable surety and concluded by saying, "These are my only
submissions."

The justice of the peace took even less time to state her ruling
that Jonathan should be released under $3,000 bail. She said he had
three things in his favour: he did not have any more charges out-
standing; his criminal record consisted of just one conviction several
years earlier and he had given himself up voluntarily to police.

Fox decided to try to salvage something from the unsuccessful
hearing by asking the justice of the peace to impose conditions on
Jonathan's release. Detective Leng, who had been in favour of
granting bail, had made out a list of conditions that he believed
should be imposed on Jonathan if he were released. Fox felt that he
should at least get the court to restrict Jonathan's freedom in the
ways that the police had suggested. The justice of the peace agreed
to this and Jonathan's release was made conditional on his living at
his home, reporting regularly to the Niagara Regional Police,
which had jurisdiction in the area where he lived, refraining from
drinking or taking drugs, not going to Hamilton except for work,
staying away from the complainant's home and not contacting her.
The justice of the peace also imposed a curfew that would require
Jonathan to be home by 10 p.m. each evening.

It did not occur to either Fox or, apparently, the justice of the
peace that there was a crucial item missing from the list of conditions. It is normal when someone is released on bail after being
charged with a serious offence involving a gun that he or she
should be prohibited from carrying a firearm. Detective Leng had
forgotten to include this in his list of conditions. It was, he subsequently admitted, a simple oversight — a mistake he should never
have made.

If Fox had been drawing up the conditions himself, he may

very well have remembered to include the firearms prohibition. It was, after all, a routine clause. But he was relying on the list that had been provided by a very experienced police officer and he was also worried about imposing on the justice of the peace, since it was her prerogative to set the conditions of bail. It is unlikely that anyone will ever know if the justice of the peace also forgot or if she had some reason for not imposing a firearm prohibition, since the law does not allow inquests to question judicial decisions and she did not come forward to provide any public explanation for her conduct at the bail hearing.

Fox was upset over the decision, but did not feel that he had grounds for appeal. He was frustrated that his planned cross-examination had not worked, that he had been thrown off by this and had failed to make his case as strongly as he should have. He later admitted that he did not subsequently discuss the case with his boss, the Hamilton-Wentworth Crown attorney, because he was a little embarrassed over his performance. He told himself that he had perhaps been wrong in believing that this was not a suitable case for bail release, since a very experienced police officer and justice of the peace had come to a different conclusion. He also took some comfort from Child's assurance that Jonathan was going to be assessed at the Clarke Institute. It was not as if they were simply releasing a violent individual onto the streets.

In fact, Jonathan was not admitted to the Clarke until June 27, nearly three weeks after the hearing. The admission was arranged through his family doctor, who reported that Jonathan seemed depressed about his situation and helpless about the future. When interviewed, Jonathan told her that he liked pornography including violence and felt ambivalent about relationships with women. He said he was afraid. "It was almost as if he wanted someone else to take charge," the doctor noted. Jonathan told her, "If somebody doesn't do something, I don't know what I might do next."

When he was first admitted to the hospital, Jonathan described himself as "intermittently hopeless and terrible." He said he had the feeling that life was over for him and "everything turns to ashes." He would not acknowledge any responsibility for the assault on April 7 and provided only very sketchy information about the events that preceded it. He said, "I knew I was doing something, but I don't know what."

It did not make sense to the hospital staff, however, that Jonathan not only claimed to have no memory of the assault, but also had no explanation as to where he obtained his weapon. Nurses and doctors soon noticed that each time he told his story he gave contradictory accounts. Dr. Peter Collins, the psychiatrist in charge of the assessment, began to suspect that something was amiss.

A social worker who interviewed Jonathan noted that all his concern about his alleged crime was focused on his own plight and that of his family. He showed no compassion for the victim. The social worker found that Jonathan's demeanour changed constantly throughout the interview, that at times he was light and engaging, while at other points he became angry. She got the impression that he was sometimes using his anger as a way of distancing himself and avoiding answering questions that he found difficult. When she asked him about sexually anomalous behaviour, he responded by suggesting that the social worker must be perverted to be asking such sick questions.

The social worker also talked to Sheila, who said that she had been "afraid something like this would happen." Sheila gave the social worker some information about Jonathan's previous violent episodes and explained that he "sometimes hates the world and everybody and wants to strike out."

A second appointment was made for Sheila to see the social worker, but Sheila cancelled it. She claimed that her babysitting arrangements had fallen through, but this seemed to run counter to the arrangement that she would bring the children in to visit with Jonathan while she saw the social worker. Sheila would later explain that she was frustrated, because she learned from the social worker that Jonathan was there only for assessment and would not be receiving any treatment at the hospital. She said she did not try to talk to doctors on the phone, because she could not afford long-distance phone calls and was busy with her children. She explained, "I had a lot of things to take care of. They were professionals. I didn't want to interfere. I thought they were looking after the situation."

The social worker did, in fact, recommend that Jonathan be offered psychiatric treatment to help manage his behaviour and deal with emotional issues. She did not believe that he would follow up on such treatment opportunities, however, because he did not indicate that he had any motivation. She noted that he appeared to demonstrate limited insight into the dynamics of his situation.

Psychiatric staff were meanwhile becoming more suspicious of Jonathan. It had been explained to him that people who experience alcoholic blackouts are still accountable for their actions, because they know what they are doing at the time, even if they cannot remember afterwards. Jonathan's response to this was to display other symptoms to psychiatrists. Dr. Collins remarked that while their mandate was to assess Jonathan, it seemed that his was to come up with symptoms that would suggest that he was not responsible for his actions.

Jonathan began to exaggerate his depression and act differently in front of staff than he did with other patients. Jonathan soon learned more about mental illness from other patients and realized that it is only psychotics, people who are judged to be out of touch with reality, who are not held responsible for their actions. He began claiming that he was hearing voices, seeing things and feeling hands tapping on shoulders. He gave doctors what Dr. Collins described as "a B-movie presentation of what a person thinks crazy people experience."

Tests were administered which indicated that Jonathan was deliberately trying to fake the results. But the tests also showed that his thinking was disturbed, that he had a poor self-image and was antisocial, that he was suspicious of but also dependent on others, and that he was impulsive and tended to become disorganized when under stress.

One set of tests was designed to determine whether he had dangerous sexual inclinations. It involved monitoring his level of sexual arousal while he was shown different visual images. He was shown a video depicting a man stalking and eventually stabbing a woman. At the point where the assailant stabbed the woman, Jonathan jumped out of his seat and let out a shout. He responded similarly to a second set of sexually violent images. Psychologists noted that he was noticeably distressed and very quiet after the tests. As he walked back to his ward he seemed to be brooding and had a frightened look in his eyes. However, the testing technique that was used was still at an experimental stage and it was not possible to determine whether or not Jonathan had sexually sadistic tendencies.

The final diagnosis of the Clarke Institute psychiatric team was that Jonathan was faking mental illness and amnesia. They did not find that he was suffering from a psychotic disorder which involved a break from reality. But they did come to the conclusion that he was a very dangerous man.

Jonathan was diagnosed as suffering from an antisocial personality disorder, impulsiveness and other symptoms detected in the tests. Personality disorders involve long-term difficulties in behaviour and relationships. They do not cloud people's reason to the point where they do not know what they are doing. Nor are they grounds for designating an accused person mentally ill in the eyes of the law.

In explaining his diagnosis at the inquest, Dr. Collins said that Jonathan "was bad, not mad." Jonathan was found to have a mixture of two types of personality disorder. One of these, which is known as a "borderline" personality disorder, caused him to be unstable and impulsive. The other was the anti-social personality disorder, which characterizes people who were previously called psychopaths or sociopaths. In most cases, something has happened in their first years of life that has impaired their ability to form bonds with other people. They are unable to feel love, remorse or a sense of responsibility for others. Such people are usually intensely selfish, manipulative individuals, who are unable to feel love, compassion or empathy.

Psychiatrists have difficulty dealing with personality disorders because they are not susceptible to being treated by drugs or psycho-therapy. In fact, they can best be treated by non-medical professionals, such as psychologists, using counselling and behavioural modification techniques to help patients understand that they need to change their behaviour and to teach them how to anticipate and avoid situations that get them into trouble. This is a very slow treatment process, which, in the case of criminal psychopaths, can best be undertaken after legal sanctions have shown patients that they must take responsibility for their behaviour and be accountable for its consequences.

It is almost impossible to help people with severe personality disorders, unless they have a very serious and persevering commitment to treatment. Unfortunately, the very same personality problems that get such people into trouble often make it almost impossible for them to recognize that they need help and then follow through with treatment. The psychologist who examined Jonathan at the Clarke noted that he seemed to be saying, "I'm very ill, mixed up and I don't need treatment." The psychologist concluded that Jonathan was "trying to have it both ways: he wanted to evade responsibility and avoid treatment."

There was no doubt that Jonathan was a dangerous man. He was manipulative, dishonest, impulsive, volatile, lacking in insight and compassion. He was not interested in getting treatment for his problems. He was clearly capable of chilling violence and possibly entertained sadistic sexual fantasies. But he was not legally insane and was not making any direct threats that he would harm himself or anyone else. This meant that he could not be held in a psychiatric hospital against his will. He was not, under the terms of the Ontario Mental Health Act, certifiably insane and the Clarke Institute therefore had no choice but to release him. The psychiatrists took the view that it was the responsibility of the criminal law and not the medical profession to protect the public from someone like Jonathan. They wondered why he was out on bail.

Dr. Collins regarded Jonathan as a "time-bomb." He warned James Child, Jonathan's lawyer, of this, but felt sure that the lawyer would not act on this information, since the lawyer, too, was bound by rules of confidentiality. If Jonathan had announced that he was going to go out and shoot somebody, the psychiatrist could have held him for a psychiatric examination and the lawyer would then have been bound to warn police. But Jonathan had made no such threat and neither he nor the psychiatrists could tell when or where his violence would next explode.

Before Jonathan left the hospital, Dr. Collins confronted him with the suggestion that he had been faking mental illness. Jonathan admitted that he had been telling half-truths, but said it was because he found it difficult to be honest, not that he was deliberately trying to deceive. Dr. Collins did not really believe this, but offered to provide ongoing counselling to Jonathan, who declined, saying that Toronto was too far from his home. Jonathan promised that he would see his family doctor for further treatment. He was still receiving anti-depressant medication, although doctors at the Clarke Institute took the view that his depression was a direct result of his problems with the law.

According to Sheila, Jonathan seemed lost when he got home. He was glad to see his children, but did not seem to know what to do with himself. Sheila had the impression that he was despondent because he did not get any treatment at the Clarke. But it is more likely that he was finally coming to terms with the fact that he was not going to be able to use psychiatric problems as an excuse, or choose treatment as an alternative to jail. He was released on

August 2, and the case was remanded until August 9. It was clear that he would soon be forced to set a date for trial.

August 9 was a Friday and Jonathan arranged an appointment with his family doctor prior to his afternoon court appearance. He wanted to get some more anti-depressant medication and a note from her stating that he was well enough to return to work. Sheila would later make much of the fact that he did not kiss each of the children when he left the house, as was his usual custom. The doctor found him agitated and depressed. He told her that he was scared of going to jail and worried that Sheila would leave him. Before giving him more medication, the doctor warned him against overdosing. He told her that he would not do that to Sheila, that he would not leave her alone with four children.

He appeared in court that afternoon. A judge agreed to his lawyer's request that the case be remanded again in order for the defence to consider the results of a psychiatric assessment. The Crown did not ask for a copy of the psychiatric report and the defence lawyer did not offer any information on it.

Sheila was worried when Jonathan did not return home after the court appearance. She checked the medicine cupboard and saw that Jonathan had taken all his remaining pills with him. Usually he took his medication at home before going to bed. She phoned the Hamilton-Wentworth Regional Police to report him missing. She asked to speak to Detective Leng, but he was off duty. Sheila told the police officer who answered the phone that she was worried that Jonathan might be sitting by the road somewhere full of pills. The officer told her that her husband was probably just out "celebrating with his buddies."

Jonathan was, in fact, at a Niagara Falls border crossing, attempting to enter the United States. He told a U.S. customs officer that he was planning to go to Key West, Florida. He was driving an old Toyota hatchback. The officer decided to search his car, observing that Jonathan seemed to have very little luggage. He found a .22 calibre rifle with two packets of ammunition.

This was not an unlawful weapon since it is commonly used for hunting. In Canada, one is required to have a licence, known as a firearms acquisition certificate, in order to buy such a gun. But this was an older weapon which may well have been purchased before the licensing system came into effect. When the customs officer appeared to be concerned about the rifle, Jonathan asked if he could just leave the gun at the border.

The officer asked Jonathan if he had ever been arrested and Jonathan said he had once been convicted of cultivating marijuana. When the officer asked if there was anything else, Jonathan said, "Do you count stuff that you haven't gone to court for yet?" He went on to explain that he was charged with uttering a death threat. He showed the customs official the bail recognizance form.

"There's a little bit more here than what you told me," said the officer after reading the document, which also listed the charges of sexual assault with a weapon and unlawful confinement.

Jonathan replied, "I didn't tell you, because I don't remember doing those things."

Realizing that he was dealing with someone who could present serious problems, the customs officer asked Jonathan to submit to a personal search. This search revealed another document which caused grave concern. In a pocket, a note was found, neatly hand-written on a sheet of lined paper.

Psychiatrists who subsequently examined the note agreed with U.S. immigration officials that it appeared to express suicidal intentions, since it described feelings of intense self-loathing and a belief that its author did not deserve to be alive. Jonathan had written his own name in brackets at the end of the note and given himself the title "Mr. Dirt." The note read:

> What the hell am I, not human anyway. Just a cheap imitation, a
> phony, nothing but a piece of shit. I don't deserve to be alive in

this world, in fact not any world. I have helped sire four beautiful children that I cannot believe could be mine, I don't feel I deserve to be their father. My life is nothing but a dream, reality is not real because it is too cruel to be true. What kind of life is this, nothing but horror. Living is not worth it, neither is death. So what the hell are we here for. It must be to see how much shit we can take. I take so much, but can't get rid of it, there's so many horrors to live through. I believe we are all flies on a piece of shit, only good enough to break down more decay. Shit is a higher level of life than I am. I am the ground that shit lies on, only to be broken down by the flies that we are. I am the great ceptic (*sic*) tank of life.

Jonathan was referred to U.S. Immigration Inspector Hugh O'Hear. After reviewing the note and the bail form and having heard about the rifle and what Jonathan said to the customs officer, it was obvious to O'Hear that this was not a person who should be allowed into the United States. Nor did he seem like someone who should be allowed to remain free in Canada, after what was obviously an attempt to skip bail. He appeared to be a suicidal, armed and dangerously unstable man.

Although it was not his responsibility to do so, O'Hear took it upon himself to inform Canadian police. This proved to be less straight-forward a task than he might have assumed. There were two different police jurisdictions involved: Hamilton-Wentworth, where the offence had taken place, and Niagara, where Jonathan lived. Niagara police referred O'Hear to Hamilton, where an officer told him that it was the Grimsby detachment of the Niagara Regional Police which was overseeing Jonathan's bail.

O'Hear spoke to a Grimsby officer, who took the position that he could do nothing, since Jonathan had not actually broken the terms of his bail. He noted that there was no condition that prohibited Jonathan from being in possession of a firearm. O'Hear pointed out that he would breach his curfew if he were allowed to proceed to Florida, but the Niagara officer's point was that he could be home by 10 p.m. if he was not allowed across the border. O'Hear was frustrated by these arguments and could not believe that it was not a crime to attempt to breach bail. In fact, he was correct. Jonathan could have been arrested on those grounds.

O'Hear hung up in frustration. The Niagara officer did decide to contact the Hamilton-Wentworth Criminal Investigation Division to alert them to the situation and to see if they wanted to take some action. The duty officer at the Hamilton C.I.D. would later maintain that he was told nothing about the gun or the note, which O'Hear described as a "suicide note." O'Hear was certain that he communicated this information, at least initially, to the Niagara police. The C.I.D. officer considered the terms of Jonathan's bail, consulted with a colleague and came to the conclusion that there was nothing that the police could do. He was apparently unaware of two separate provisions of the Criminal Code of Canada which allow police to arrest a person whom they have reason to believe may be about to breach a bail recognizance. He telephoned O'Hear and told him brusquely that there was nothing the police could do about Jonathan Yeo, because he had not broken his curfew.

By this time, O'Hear had given up on the police and was trying to interest the Canadian border officials in at least confiscating the rifle. U.S. customs regulations required that the rifle be returned to Jonathan, since it was not a prohibited weapon under United States law. O'Hear noted that Jonathan had gone through several mood swings during the two hours that he was being detained at the border station, and that now he was relatively quiet and compliant. However, it did not make any sense to allow him to take his gun back into Canada.

O'Hear had the idea that Canada customs officials could ask to see his licence and then confiscate the gun if he did not produce one. He telephoned the customs office on the other side of the international bridge. The woman who answered the phone refused to talk to him, simply passing his call on to a Canada immigration official. The reason for this was that, in the minds of customs officials, Jonathan had never left Canada, as he had been refused admission to the United States. They therefore believed that they had no right to question Jonathan and thus no grounds for confiscating his weapon.

By an absurd quirk of bureaucratic thinking, the Immigration Department took a different view and therefore believed that it was their business to talk to someone who had been refused entry to the United States. The problem was that since Jonathan was a Canadian citizen there was actually nothing that the immigraiton officials would be able to do to stop him from returning home.

O'Hear was referred to Alexander Welsh, who was the senior Canadian immigration officer on duty at the border post that day. He told Welsh about the gun and the ammunition, read him the suicide note and explained that the police had shown no interest whatsoever in this man. Welsh conducted a record search to make sure that he was a Canadian citizen and not wanted by police. He decided there was no point in talking to the police himself, because, as he later explained, "If police weren't interested, they weren't interested. They get pretty frustrated if you bug them. We don't always get along."

Then Welsh came up with what he would describe as his "game plan." It was a plan that was solely designed to protect personnel at the border post from a dangerous man who was armed and emotionally disturbed. Welsh was the only immigration official on duty with 11 customs officers. The customs officers were mostly women and many of them were students. None of the border personnel was armed. The normal procedure for dealing with a person who is refused entry to the United States is for customs officers to talk to the person and immediately refer him or her to an immigration officer. If the person is a Canadian citizen, the immigration officer is not in a position to refuse entry to Canada.

Welsh's plan was that the customs officers should stay in the building or hide in their booths while he went out to talk to Jonathan in his car. He would question him as little as possible, so as not to disturb him, and quickly send him on his way. This is what was done. Customs officers with walkie-talkies stood on the bridge in order to spot Jonathan's car as it made its way across. The customs officers then took refuge and watched from a distance, while Welsh approached the car and asked Jonathan for proof of his citizenship. The supervisor of the customs officers later explained that they were very cautious because they were concerned that he was unstable and might shoot somebody. But she said they had no mandate to try to take away his gun, since he had not left Canada, according to customs regulations.

It was about 7:30 p.m. when Jonathan was sent on his way by the cautious Canadian border guards. From the bridge in Niagara Falls, it is about a 45-minute drive to Burlington. Perhaps Jonathan had it in his mind to drive to eastern Ontario or Quebec and try to cross at one of the less frequented border posts. If so, Burlington was directly along his route.

At about 9 p.m. that night, Jonathan was seen in Tequila Willie's, the tavern on the South Service Road just off the main highway in Burlington. The doorman at the bar thought he recognized Jonathan, but when he got close, he realized that he was mistaken. The doorman later identified Jonathan from newspaper photographs. He remembered him because of his cold stare. Jonathan continued to stare at the doorman as he made his way out of the bar. The doorman saw him standing outside by his brown Toyota, still staring coldly at the door of the tavern.

A few hundred yards away at about the same time, a young woman with curly blonde hair walked out of the Cedar Springs Racquet Club and began to jog along the South Service Road.

Part Three
A MURDEROUS RAMPAGE

nine

DISAPPEARANCE
AND SEARCH

▼

N INA HAD ARRANGED TO MEET her father after the tennis tournament on August 9, because she did not like driving alone
at night. When he finished his game, Rocco waited for her in the
racquet club coffee shop. When Nina failed to show up, he checked
at the front desk and found that she had left her car keys there. She
had not left a message and Rocco was anxious. After phoning
Priscilla at home and learning that Nina was not there, he walked
around the club looking for her and asked one of the female
employees to search the ladies' locker rooms.

It was very unusual for Nina to go anywhere without telling
her parents where she would be and she was usually reliable about
keeping appointments, even if she did tend to be late. It was particularly concerning that she did not have her purse, which she had
left in the car. She had apparently gone off somewhere without her
keys and she may not have been carrying any cash.

Nevertheless, she was a 19-year-old woman who certainly had
no obligation to inform her parents of what she was doing at all
times. She may well have spontaneously decided to go out with a
friend, after discovering that she would not be playing tennis that
evening. There had obviously been some mix-up in communications at the tennis club already over the time of Nina's game, so it
was possible that Nina had left a message that Rocco never

received. It was not clear why she left her keys for him.

At this stage, Rocco was more alarmed than Priscilla, who urged her husband to drive home in Nina's car. Priscilla assumed that Nina must have returned to the Festival of Friends, where she had been working as a volunteer earlier that day. There was clearly nothing that her parents could do at 11 p.m. on a Friday night, except wait and hope for the best.

Rocco fell asleep, while Priscilla sat up painting and listening for the phone or for the sound of Nina returning. She eventually went to bed and fell into a doze, from which she awoke at about 2 a.m. with the sickening realization that she had not heard Nina come in. Nina had never stayed out all night without telling her parents. Priscilla got up to check Nina's bedroom. Finding it empty, Priscilla looked around the rest of the house and then woke Rocco, who was also convinced that there may be grounds for concern. After phoning Nina's friends, none of whom had any idea where she could be, Rocco and Priscilla drove to the park in Hamilton where the festival was being held. The park was deserted and they disconsolately searched among the darkened tents, booths and stages that had been erected for the festival.

Now convinced that something had happened to Nina, Rocco and Priscilla returned home and phoned the police. They were told that no one meeting Nina's description had been reported as being involved in an accident. The police were reluctant to file a missing persons report at that stage, since they felt that it would not be unusual for a 19-year-old woman to spend the night with a boyfriend without informing her parents.

Etienne was roused by his parents and he phoned Nina's friend Chris Forrest, who had been with her the previous evening at the Festival of Friends. Chris was extremely worried. It was, in his view, almost inconceivable that Nina would have gone off somewhere without telling her parents. He and other friends used to tease Nina about how she always insisted on going home early or phoning to tell her parents where she was. Chris said that he would go to the park and conduct a more thorough search. Chris's sense of the gravity of the situation was reinforced by his mother's reaction when he woke her to ask if he could borrow the car. At first she sleepily waved him away, but sat bolt upright when he explained the reason. She began to cry.

Meanwhile, the de Villiers continued to phone friends, hospitals and emergency services. They returned to the tennis club, which was locked up for the night, and searched the grounds with a flashlight. As dawn was breaking, they tried again to persuade the police to launch a search. The circumstances of Nina's disappearance were alarming to the de Villiers and to Nina's friends. But there was, as yet, nothing to cause police undue concern. The Halton police force received more than 800 reports of missing persons a year and almost all of them were eventually located with an innocent explanation for their disappearance. An officer from the Halton Regional Police, which covers Burlington and neighbouring communities to the north and east, agreed to fill out a missing person report. This report would be broadcast to all Halton police vehicles and filed in the computerized records of the Canadian Police Information Centre. But the officer explained that the police force would not initiate an active search unless some evidence was found to suggest that there had been foul play.

Feeling helpless and desperately afraid for Nina, Rocco and Priscilla decided that they should get a private security company to investigate, if the police refused to do so. They phoned the organization "Child Find" for advice on this and a local representative visited their home immediately to offer comfort and support. Priscilla phoned some security and investigation agencies, but was frustrated because their offices were not yet open. She also kept phoning the tennis club to see if any of the staff had arrived for work.

Eventually, Priscilla was able to contact people at the tennis club, who responded with horror and alarm. They volunteered to search the grounds as well as the buildings immediately. Priscilla explained that any clue to Nina's disappearance might be helpful in getting the police involved.

Soon after 9 a.m., a fitness instructor at the club discovered a distinctive multi-coloured headband on the ground beside a willow tree at the rear of the building. Priscilla identified it as one belonging to Nina and immediately called the police, whose attitude changed abruptly. Although the situation looked bleaker than ever, Priscilla felt immensely relieved by the dispatch and efficiency with which the police now responded as they took control of the situation.

When they arrived at the club, police officers discovered that there was a disturbed area near the willow tree, by the back end of the parking lot. It was a large tree with branches that hung nearly to the ground. Under it there appeared to be spots of blood on a stone and on some leaves. There were several tire tracks in the mud at the edge of the parking lot and running towards them from the willow tree was a set of parallel scuff marks in the soil, such as might have been made by the feet of someone who was being dragged along the ground.

These discoveries prompted the police to launch a major operation, calling in 26 officers and establishing a command post in a nearby public works building. The racquet club and surrounding area were searched more thoroughly and Nina's movements on the previous evening were pieced together through interviews with family, friends and racquet club staff. Search efforts were hampered by a violent rain storm which flooded the area where the ground had been disturbed.

It was not until 6:30 p.m. that the Halton police issued an alert to all police forces in the surrounding area saying that Nina was believed to have been abducted. The officer who eventually took charge of the investigation was at a loss when asked at the inquest to explain the delay in issuing this message. He speculated that the officers at the scene were too busy searching and interviewing witnesses to think about issuing an alert. They may also have believed that they did not have enough information to make such a message worthwhile, since Nina's description would fit many young women and there was no clue about the identity and whereabouts of her abductor.

Many police officers would remain unaware of the alert, anyway, since it had been issued with instructions that it not be broadcast over the radio. The reason for this is that the abductor might have been listening in on police radio frequencies and have gained valuable information about how much, or how little, the police knew. In the Halton region, where all police cars were equipped with computer terminals, the message would be readily available. But police forces not equipped with such technology would have to rely on reading the message to officers when they began their shifts. The rationale for not broadcasting the message was difficult to understand in view of the fact that a press release was sent out at almost exactly the same time as the alert was issued.

Ten days later it would become clear that the delay in getting the message out to other police forces could have had no impact on Nina's fate. But there was a chance that another life could have been saved if Jonathan had been apprehended sooner.

On the day after she disappeared, however, and throughout the following week, her family and friends had to assume that Nina was alive and probably being held captive somewhere. Since no eyewitnesses had come forward and little evidence was left at the scene, the best chance of rescuing her seemed to lie in someone recognizing her from a picture or description and observing or remembering something. It seemed vital therefore to spread the word of Nina's disappearance as widely and as quickly as possible. Even though she and Rocco were by inclination very private people, Priscilla went out of her way to court the media, exposing her anguish to reporters, cameras and microphones in order to promote awareness of Nina's plight.

While the de Villiers had to cling to the faint hope that Nina might still be alive, they could derive no comfort whatsoever from any evidence that had been gathered. The headband, the drag marks and the blood stains all pointed quite clearly to a dreadful crime. As no more concrete evidence emerged during the following week, they were all forced to live in an emotional hinterland, unable to give full reign to grief or despair, but finding it harder to hope as each day went by.

Priscilla was determined to remain strong and in control. She was tireless in dealing with the media and the stream of friends, neighbours and well-wishers who began coming to the house as soon as the news of Nina's disappearance broke. A friend, who talked to her on the Sunday after the abduction, noted that she was apparently still in shock, talking like a robot and showing no emotion as she recounted the events of the previous two days. It was only at night, when she could not sleep and was left alone with her thoughts, that Priscilla allowed herself to cry.

Rocco and Etienne responded differently. Rocco, who was usually calm and reserved, often seemed to be prostrated with grief and afraid of losing his sanity. A friend who visited the house described him as crumbling into her arms with such abandon that she could not hold him up. On the other hand, friends were worried about Etienne because he was inclined to withdraw into silence and abstract himself from the situation. He seemed inaccessible and inconsolable. He answered the door to one family friend, who came to give her condolence, and just stood there silently, his hands extended in a gesture of helplessness and despair.

Priscilla, Rocco and Etienne were each afraid of upsetting one another more by speaking of what was on their minds. It seemed impossible to communicate bleak emotions and dreadful speculations without exacerbating each other's pain and trepidation. They were a close family and normally would discuss issues and problems together, but now this normal interaction was lost. They each found that they needed to be with other people outside the family, with whom they could share their grief, anger, confusion and disbelief.

In fact, the de Villiers' need for company was immediately answered by a corresponding need among all Nina's friends and acquaintances, as well as neighbours and strangers, who felt touched by what had happened. As soon as the facts of Nina's disappearance became known in the community, people began to demonstrate the kind of commitment and concern that would later give rise to a grass-roots campaign against violence. People who knew Nina and valued her were devastated by her disappearance, while others saw her abduction as a violation of their community. Many people in the neighbourhood had seen Nina and her parents out together and regarded them as a close and happy family. They identified with the de Villiers as parents and now felt that their own families were also at risk. Their community no longer seemed safe. Many of these people felt a need to express these emotions and act upon them. The obvious way to do that was to visit the de Villiers home with offers of help and condolence.

Some of the people who visited the de Villiers during the days that followed Nina's disappearance found that they could help in practical ways. These people included two women from the racquet club who would later become founding members of CAVEAT, the group which lobbied for changes in the light of Nina's death. Dorothy Leonard and Judy Gordon took on the job of handling phone calls and helping to deal with the media on the family's behalf. They were surprised to find that media representatives were for the most part responsible and showed respect toward the family. They were also impressed with the fact that Priscilla and Rocco gave a lot of consideration to what they wanted to say and were always conscious of the impact of what was happening on the community. At one point, Priscilla was anxious that the racquet club might get bad publicity as a result of what happened and went out of her way to point out that the club was in no way to blame.

As news of Nina's disappearance spread, more and more visitors appeared at the de Villiers' home. Doctors and nurses from Rocco's hospital, teachers from Nina's school, her friends, their parents, people from the yacht club, the tennis club, members of Nina's choirs, students and faculty from McMaster University and hundreds of strangers would come to the door. Many of these visitors were surprised to find that they were welcomed into the home, when they had expected simply to deliver flowers or a card, mumble their condolences and leave.

Close friends were amazed at this phenomenon, especially as many of them had been shy about visiting because they knew that the de Villiers tended to be very private people. Priscilla's friend Cathy Crowder subsequently exclaimed, "It was like pilgrimages to Mecca. The whole world was coming over. I thought it was nuts. I couldn't believe it. I've never seen so much food in my life — and flowers and notes stuck in the door. People would come all day long and I'd joke about it to Priscilla and say, 'I'm going to have to leave because there are no chairs left. Even your enemies are coming.'"

Nina's closest friends refused to give up hope as long as there was a faint chance that she was alive. They responded with the same efficiency and resourcefulness that they had shown working with Nina on school projects. They organized a massive poster and media campaign to keep Nina's image and description in the public eye.

Sheila Singh described how she responded to news of Nina's disappearance. At first, she was in a state of shock and she just did not want to believe that it could have happened. She was alone in her parents' house and, when her father arrived home, she threw herself into his arms saying, "Daddy, Nina's gone." Sheila thought of herself as an idealist and was often teased by her friends for taking a rosy view of the world. But suddenly, she was starkly aware that circumstances of Nina's disappearance were such that she was unlikely to be found alive.

Chris Forrest, like many other friends of Nina, felt that he had to believe that Nina was alive and act on that belief. He did not even want to think about what might be happening to her, if she were alive, because that too was painful. He and his friends concentrated only on their desperate wish that she be alive and safe, as they worked around the clock to mobilize a search.

They found out that Child Find had produced some posters bearing a description of Nina and a print of the photograph that she had taken just a week earlier for her international driver's licence. However, the posters were only going to be made available to people who phoned Child Find to request them. Chris, who had organized poster campaigns to promote the Festival of Friends, went much further than that and got permission from Child Find to take over the production and distribution of posters.

Telephone companies, printers and computer stores were persuaded to donate services or lend equipment for free. Nina's friends David Bruckmann and J.P. Timmerman worked overnight to make a computerized image of the photograph. They incorporated this in a redesigned poster, which they sent across the country via fax modems. Chris drew up a plan for the distribution of posters in the Hamilton and Burlington areas, dividing the cities into zones in order to use resources most effectively and avoid duplication. Another friend wrote a set of guidelines, specifying the kinds of locations in which the posters should be placed, how store or restaurant owners should be approached and how questions should be fielded. Cellular telephones were borrowed in order to ensure that the young people would feel safe while distributing posters and could phone for help at any time. By Thursday, August 15, six days after Nina's disappearance, 7,000 posters had been printed and put on display in the city of Hamilton alone.

Sheila Singh, who felt she had no special skills to offer to the poster campaign, decided that her role should be to cook for the de Villiers, their visitors and the volunteers who were working on the search. She and two other friends of Nina, Sarah Penvidic and Mudita Bhargava, took turns running the kitchen. One day, they and Etienne made pizza for 80 people and, on another occasion, they made chicken for 40. Sheila later explained, "I knew they didn't want food. I know that they didn't feel like eating. But it was all I could do to try to keep comfort in the house. I tried to smile. I put on funny make-up. I put on bright clothes. I went over there and I smiled."

The bold front that Nina's friends put on could not hide how much they were suffering. Priscilla was pained by this and did what she could to help. Many young people who went to the house thinking they were there to comfort the family were surprised to find that they ended up being the ones who were comforted. Two of Rocco's colleagues who specialized in bereavement counselling volunteered to talk to some of the kids and help them. A teacher from Hillfield also visited the house regularly and spent hours talking to Nina's friends, as they struggled with the gradual realization that Nina would probably not be found alive. Some gave full vent to their sorrow, anger and confusion, while others, like Etienne, seemed to keep it all inside.

What affected Sheila Singh most strongly were the comments of some of the boys, who felt guilty about their passive acceptance of sexual violence. They talked about the violent thoughts that sometimes invaded their own adolescent fantasies and explained, according to Sheila's synopsis, "We feel like we can't touch another girl, because we're afraid that they are going to fear us for the rest of their lives. We're scared of touching them or pushing them or doing anything because sometimes we have violent thoughts. We're scared because we feel like monsters."

It was comforting for Priscilla to see how deeply people cared about her daughter. Often people whom she did not even know would appear at the house, overcome with grief. A Vietnamese immigrant named Bruce was one such visitor. He was a weight-lifter, a huge young man with a gentle manner whom Nina had been tutoring through his chemistry class at university. He told Priscilla, when he arrived at the door, "I know you." Priscilla was mystified and he went on to explain, "Nina always talked about you." Bruce lived in Niagara Falls and had been intensely distressed, but was unable to find anyone with whom he could share his sorrow. He was so upset that he found it hard to talk and explained that he had almost had an accident as he drove to the de Villiers' home. Priscilla introduced him to one of the grief counsellors, who helped him to calm down and deal with his pain.

The de Villiers were given some comfort by the arrival of Priscilla's sister from South Africa and brother, an orthopedic surgeon in Timmins, Ontario. They tried to manage what had become a chaotic situation in the house and made efforts to limit the times when visitors were received. But by now people were coming from far and wide, some of them moved to sympathy because they too had lost loved ones as a result of violent crime. The de Villiers and their relatives found it difficult to turn anyone away. One of Rocco's uncles, a retired police officer, also visited from South Africa. He gave Priscilla his realistic assessment of the situation and told her that she should brace herself for the discovery of Nina's body.

The police had been conducting an intense investigation, but had come up with few promising leads. The area of the racquet club had been searched with metal detectors, dogs and a helicopter equipped with sensors to detect heat from a shallow grave. But no trace of Nina or her abductor had been found. As a result of widespread publicity given to the case, hundreds of people phoned police with information and tips. These scraps of information were fed into a computer program called "Holmes," which is designed to assist police in managing major cases.

Gradually, information was compiled about people who had been seen near the racquet club on the night that Nina disappeared. A list of suspects was beginning to materialize. Information also began to emerge which caused Jonathan Yeo to be added to the list. But, with no material evidence linking him or any other suspect to Nina's abduction, police efforts remained focused on looking for Nina or for any evidence which might suggest what had happened to her.

The Halton police put out an appeal for members of the public to help with an intensive search of the area around the racquet club. It was not until then that anyone fully comprehended the intensity of the public concern that the case had generated. More than 5,000 people showed up for the search, causing organizational problems for the police, who had not anticipated such numbers.

For Nina's friends, the search was an agonizing ordeal. Cynthia Kerr, who wrote the song about the Montreal massacre that Nina helped record, joined the search because she felt it was something that she should do, although she had hardly eaten or slept since she heard the news of Nina's disappearance. She felt terrified as she listened to a policeman explaining what evidence to look for. Then, as she walked in a straight line alongside other searchers, Cynthia was scared that she might find a piece of Nina's clothing. She had come to search, but she did not want to look.

Many people in the community were feeling helpless and afraid. This was the second abduction of a teenager from Burlington that summer and in the previous case the victim's body had been found cut into pieces and encased in concrete blocks at the bottom of a lake. People were afraid to let their kids walk the streets at night and many young people were feeling angry that they were forced to become prisoners in their own homes.

The police held a public information meeting on the evening after the search. About 1,000 people attended and they wanted to know if there might be a serial killer in their midst. The police could only tell them that they did not know. Some people in the crowd responded with anger and extreme frustration. There were open threats of vigilantism and the chief of police issued stern warnings about the danger of citizens taking the law into their own hands.

Priscilla and Rocco were extremely disturbed by vengeful feelings that were expressed at the meeting. There appeared to be a real danger of violence if someone were to be mistaken for the abductor. They were reminded of what happened to their neighbourhood in Cape Town when rioting broke out. It seemed to the de Villiers that once again they were living in a community where people no longer believed that the rule of law could protect them and had come to fear that nobody was safe.

Two days later, a friend and colleague of Rocco contacted the media to issue a statement on his behalf. She said that the family was hoping that the community could stay healthy and channel its energies in positive ways. "Dr. de Villiers wants very much that people not be frightened, that people should feel very secure, not only because that's his belief but also because it was his daughter's."

Nina's friends continued to work on their poster campaign and also contacted radio and television stations to persuade them to run public service messages and news items about the search. On the Saturday, eight days after Nina's disappearance, they began what was to have been a poster blitz in Toronto. They had 10,000 new posters printed and had set up their headquarters in office space that had been loaned to them. But they found it difficult to persuade people to put up posters and concentrated their efforts on media publicity. Then they received news that a body had been found.

The police contacted the de Villiers early on Saturday morning to inform them that a woman's body had been discovered floating in a creek near Kingston, Ontario. There was no clothing on the body, which had decomposed so that it was not easy to identify.

The police were asking whether Nina wore nail polish and if she had her ears pierced. They said they could not identify the body, until an orthodontist had examined the dead woman's jaw.

Even after they received the news, some of Nina's friends were still holding out hope. Chris heard about the discovery from another friend, who told him that it was probably not Nina, because the woman in the water had dark hair and freckles. Chris, who had studied forensic anthropology at university, knew that hair turns darker on a body that is exposed to water and that blood pockets that look like freckles can form under the skin. He kept this knowledge to himself. He told friends, who asked his opinion about the body, that they should not waste time speculating. He said, "Every minute is potentially the last minute of her life. We can't stop searching until we get 100 percent proof that she is dead."

The de Villiers had agreed to go with friends to spend the weekend in Kingston, where the kids from the sailing school were participating in a regatta. It had seemed like a good idea to get everyone out of the house. They decided to stick to this plan, in spite of the grim news they'd received. But they were on edge all the time they were in Kingston and anxious to return home, even though they knew that they would probably be going back to face bad news.

It was on the afternoon of Sunday, August 18, nine days after Nina had disappeared, that Detective Inspector Les Graham of the Halton Regional Police informed the de Villiers that the body had been identified as Nina by means of dental records and that she had been killed by a single gunshot wound to the back of her head. He was able to offer them the small consolation that death would have been instantaneous and that there was no evidence of sexual assault.

The family attempted to ensure that Nina's friends were personally informed that her body had been found. This was not always possible and many of them saw the news on television or heard it on the radio. One friend, Cynthia Kerr, was singing in a club when she caught a glimpse of Nina's picture on a television screen at the bar. She phoned the television station to find out what had happened and someone in the newsroom casually gave her a detailed account of the condition of the body. Hysterical from grief, she angrily told the television reporter that Nina was her friend and it was callous of him to have answered so off-handedly. His only response was to ask if she would hold the line while he went to get a tape recorder so that he could interview her.

It is difficult to imagine ever coming to terms with the death of a child, but it seemed to Priscilla that it would be easier to comprehend a natural or even an accidental death. There was nothing natural in Nina's death, nor was there any rational explanation for it. It was not something that happened as a consequence of anything that Nina had done or failed to do. Nina's death was something that did not seem to relate to anything in her life and in the world in which she had grown up. It seemed impossible to understand how someone could have selected Nina and deliberately chosen to frighten, hurt and kill her. Her murder was an assault on the values and beliefs of her family and her community.

Yet, Nina's family and friends were determined to remember her by asserting the values that she lived for. Instead of a funeral, a concept which would not have fit Nina's religious beliefs, they organized what was described as "a service of remembrance in celebration of her life." It was held on August 24 in St. Paul's Presbyterian Church in Hamilton, where Nina used to sing in the choir. Eight-hundred-and-fifty people crowded into the church and hundreds more gathered in an adjoining hall and on the lawn outside. Another well-attended memorial service was held at McMaster University.

At the beginning of the St. Paul's service, a recording of Nina's own singing was played. It was a tape of her Ontario Academic Credit examination performance and it included music which ranged from German *Lieder* to Duke Ellington. A similarly eclectic range of music was performed at the service, each piece having been carefully chosen to reflect Nina's tastes and values. The Reverend Willard Pottinger told the congregation, "This is not a funeral or memorial service. It is not a forum for moral outrage or social justice. It is a celebration." He reminded people that Nina tried to include more and more people in her circle of friends. He suggested that circle widened even more with her death, as an entire community expressed its grief and got involved in the search. The minister urged everyone to "stay in the circle and celebrate her life."

Etienne, one of Nina's teachers and two of her friends spoke at the service about their memories of Nina. They all recounted anecdotes that illustrated her humour, creativity and other qualities. Sheila Singh delivered one of these addresses, which she concluded by saying, "Long after these days are over, it is not their fear and horror that I will recollect. I will always remember the inescapable joy of knowing Nina. Thousands of people recognized this joy and came together to act upon the same beliefs that Nina exemplified in her life. I am amazed by the love that surrounded us all through this time and I am filled with hope and faith in a humanity that responds with such genuine compassion."

ten

A FULL
INVESTIGATION

▼

S HEILA YEO WAS THE first person to suspect that Jonathan might have something to do with Nina's abduction. Sheila would later admit that she felt a knot in her stomach when she first heard the news that a young woman had disappeared soon after Jonathan had gone missing.

Sheila had called the Niagara police on the morning after Jonathan left and an officer was sent to her home. Sheila told him about the charges that her husband was facing. She explained that her husband attacked his alleged victim and held her hostage for eight hours with a knife because he felt inferior to women. The officer was alarmed enough by this information that he asked questions about Jonathan's whereabouts at the time of the disappearance of Leslie Mahaffy, the teenager whose dismembered body was found in a lake. Sheila told him that Jonathan had been in the Clarke Institute at that time.

The officer asked Sheila if she was concerned for her own safety. She replied that she was not, but was worried that Jonathan might harm himself. This concern was noted in a missing person report that the officer subsequently filed. Neither he nor Sheila knew anything about Jonathan being turned away from the United States border with a rifle and a suicide note. There was no record of this incident on the Niagara police files. Although Jonathan had breached his bail conditions by staying out overnight, the Niagara police officer believed that it was up to the Hamilton-Wentworth Regional Police to decide whether a charge should be laid.

Brian Leng, the Hamilton-Wentworth detective who had arrested Jonathan three months earlier, heard when he got into work that morning that Sheila had tried to reach him the night before. After talking to Sheila, he decided to put out a radio bulletin requesting all Hamilton-Wentworth police patrols to look out for Jonathan's car, a brown 1982 Toyota Corona hatchback. The bulletin asked that Jonathan's whereabouts be reported. It advised officers to use caution as the suspect may be armed and dangerous or suicidal. Leng also took the precaution of warning Alison, whom Jonathan attacked in April, and suggested she move out of her apartment for the weekend.

Leng was also unaware of the border incident. The sergeant on duty the night before, who had made the decision not to have Jonathan arrested at the border, had sent off a report, which should have been delivered to Leng by courier first thing in the morning. He did not, in fact, receive it until two days later. Nevertheless, after talking to Sheila on August 10, Leng was aware that Jonathan had breached his bail conditions by failing to observe the curfew. This would have provided valid grounds for issuing a warrant for Jonathan's arrest. But Leng decided not to seek a warrant. It would have involved a great deal of paperwork and he had other cases that demanded his attention.

Subsequently, Leng was forced to acknowledge that issuing a warrant at that time for Jonathan's arrest could conceivably have saved another life. Leng recalled hearing about Nina's abduction, but he did not connect it with Jonathan's disappearance.

Jonathan did not become the prime suspect in Nina's death until a week later, when her body was discovered and examined. Police had gathered a lot of information by then about Jonathan's movements in what proved to be the last few days of his life.

Nina had last been seen jogging at 9:25 p.m. on August 9. At that point she was apparently half-way around her second circuit of the 2-kilometre block on which the Cedar Springs Racquet Club was located. It would be reasonable to assume that her murderer either followed her to the racquet club parking lot or waited for her there, having watched her set off 20 minutes earlier. Jonathan would probably have appealed to Nina for help, pretending that he was injured or lost. Nina was a very considerate young woman and would be susceptible to such an approach. A few minutes earlier, she had interrupted her run in order to give directions to a couple whom she met on the road.

Investigators concluded that Jonathan probably shot and killed Nina under the willow tree where several spots of blood were found. She would have died instantly from the bullet which penetrated the back of her neck just beneath the skull and shattered her spine. Such a wound would have caused very little bleeding. It was described by the pathologist as an "execution-style" contact wound. The muzzle of the gun was pressed against Nina's neck and her body would have acted like a silencer, muffling the sound of the gun, so that it could easily have been mistaken for the sound of a car engine backfiring.

Blood stains were subsequently found on the rear seat of Jonathan's car, suggesting that he had lain the body there, after dragging it from underneath the tree. If Nina had still been alive when she was placed in the back of the car, she would have bled more profusely than the stains indicated.

It is impossible to say what transpired between the murderer and his victim before Nina was shot. There was no other injury nor any evidence to indicate that she was sexually assaulted. During previous assaults, Jonathan's victims were usually able to save their lives by responding aggressively and using their wits. But Jonathan's fuse was shorter now. He was more desperate and more careless. Faced with the prospect of a long prison term, Jonathan was determined never again to leave a witness. Perhaps his prime motive was to punish another young woman for what Alison had done in standing up to him and reporting him to the police. There was probably nothing that Nina could have done to save her life.

Whatever happened in the parking lot and under the willow tree did not take very long, since Jonathan was seen driving away from the area of the racquet club at some time between 9:30 p.m. and 10 p.m. Jonathan and his car were identified from a very detailed description provided by another motorist whom he passed on the inside at a red light. Jonathan gave the other driver a long, cold stare before racing away. The witness did not see anyone else in the car and noticed that Jonathan had both hands on the steering wheel. These observations lent support to the theory that Nina was lying in the back, already dead or, at least, unconscious. The witness told police that he had the impression that this man was running away from something.

Nina's body was found floating in the still waters of a creek under a bridge just off Highway 401, between Napanee and Kingston. It became clear from other evidence that Jonathan was heading towards New Brunswick and this was probably the first spot on his route that appeared suitable to dispose the body. It was 286 kilometres east of Burlington, but prior to that Jonathan would have been driving through populated and well-travelled areas. There were few previous opportunities to get off the highway to an isolated location and this was the first that he might easily have spotted in advance. As Jonathan drove down a long incline leading to the Highway 133 exit, he would have been able to see the bridge where a small sideroad crossed the creek and would have noticed that there were no houses nearby.

The creek was just three metres deep, but the body was not discovered until Friday, August 16. A couple from a nearby village had stopped at the bridge to examine the railings which had been painted a week earlier. They leaned over to see how well the side of the bridge had been painted and observed the body lying face down in the water. When police investigated the scene, they found some blood spots on the ground and some hairs stuck to the freshly painted railings. Also found on the bridge were some Number 7 brand cigarette tubes, used to make homemade cigarettes, a package of which was found in the back of Jonathan's car.

After disposing of Nina's body, Jonathan continued to drive east along the highway. On the day after Nina was murdered, he arrived in the small town of Sackville, New Brunswick, close to the border of Nova Scotia. Ten years earlier, Jonathan and Sheila had gone on a camping trip to the Maritimes and their car had broken down in Sackville. A local man named Alan Gilroy had gone to their assistance, allowing them to camp overnight on his property while their car was being repaired. Gilroy never saw or heard from the Yeos after this one very casual contact. But at about 8 p.m. on Saturday, August 10, Jonathan showed up on his doorstep.

Jonathan told Gilroy that his wife and family were attending a Christian retreat in the Hamilton area and that he had decided to go to Montreal to purchase some white-faced cattle. He told an elaborate story about how he wanted to expand his hobby farm and how the cattle were going to cost him $30,000, but that the deal could not be finalized until after the weekend. He said that he had decided, while he was waiting to drive down to Moncton, New Brunswick (more than 1,000 kilometres from Montreal), to visit friends of his wife. Jonathan said that his wife's friends had not been home, so he decided to look Gilroy up in Sackville (88 kilometres beyond Moncton).

Gilroy and his wife invited Jonathan in and allowed him to sleep on their couch after spending the evening together, talking and drinking beer. They found Jonathan nervous and edgy, but there was nothing specific in his behaviour that gave them any qualms about letting him stay. They subsequently told police that he behaved well with their children, lowering his voice whenever he used swear words in front of them. Jonathan told the Gilroys that he was on medication and very tired because he had not slept for 42 hours. He continued to hang around the Gilroys' home for much of the next day and they began to feel uneasy about him, because the stories that he told about his farm, his wife and his trip kept changing. They were relieved when he left at about 3 p.m. on Sunday. He said he was heading back to Montreal to close his cattle deal.

About half-an-hour later, a motorist had a confrontation on a nearby highway with a man driving a brown Toyota Corona. The Toyota driver apparently felt that he had been cut off and aggressively overtook him before slowing down suddenly. The two drivers exchanged angry glares, but there was something about the Toyota driver that made the other motorist acutely uneasy. He backed away from any further confrontation and made a mental note of the licence number, 222 LED. The other motorist remembered it vividly, because it made him think of a .22 calibre rifle and lead bullets.

At about the same time that Jonathan was driving towards Moncton, a Canadian National Railway traffic controller was ending her shift at the Moncton rail yards. Twenty-eight-year-old Karen Marquis met her husband, Neil, before going home. Neil also worked for CN and was set to begin his shift at 4 p.m., as Karen finished hers. She told her husband that she was not going to visit her parents on the way home, as was her usual practice. She said she planned to rent a couple of videos for the evening.

An hour later, one of Karen's cousins drove by the Marquis home, located on the Trans Canada Highway about 20 minutes west of Moncton near the small town of Petitcodiac. The cousin noticed that Karen's car was not in the driveway, but there was a brown vehicle parked beside the house in the spot where her car usually stood. Later that night, when Neil Marquis returned home, Karen's car would be in the driveway, but not parked in its usual spot. A piece of cardboard, subsequently discovered in Jonathan's car, bore the handwritten message, "My car is broken down. Went to Moncton."

Perhaps Jonathan had set an ambush after watching Karen arrive at her house and then leave again to run an errand. He may have approached her with a story about his car breaking down and then returned later. One can only speculate on the basis of the pattern of his previous behaviour, a pattern which should by then have been a matter of public record, but tragically was not. What is known for certain is that he broke in by smashing a downstairs window at the side of the house.

When Neil Marquis arrived home shortly after midnight on August 12, 1991, his wife did not answer his greeting and he noticed that coffee had been spilled on the kitchen floor. Assuming that Karen must be downstairs watching videos, he went down to the finished basement where the VCR and monitor were switched on, but with no tape playing. As he went to look for her in the bedroom, he stumbled over an object in the upstairs hallway. It was the naked body of Karen Marquis, completely covered by blankets. She had been shot in the head with a rifle at close range.

Royal Canadian Mounted Police were summoned and immediately began the kind of intensive investigation with which police forces always respond to murder. Police and forensic labs tend to give priority to murder cases, sometimes at the expense of other crimes, such as sexual assaults, that are considered less serious. The testimony of a live victim is frequently considered to be less reliable than that of a corpse. Yet, it is likely that neither Karen Marquis or Nina de Villiers would have died if the Hamilton-Wentworth Regional Police or Niagara Regional Police had taken Jonathan's earlier attacks on women more seriously.

Investigators discovered similar fingerprints on both sides of a piece of broken glass. It was likely that the prints were formed when the criminal removed the glass in order to gain entry through the window. The prints were flown to Ottawa and hand-delivered to the RCMP headquarters, where a computer search was immediately conducted. They were matched with Jonathan's prints and the results relayed back to the RCMP in Moncton within two hours. In contrast, it had taken three weeks to match Jonathan's prints with those on the wine glass at Alison's apartment.

A preliminary examination of the body and the scene of the crime revealed no evidence that the victim had been sexually assaulted. But forensic tests of vaginal and rectal swabs subsequently detected semen in both and identified the semen as Jonathan's. A bullet hole was found in a night table beside the bed, indicating that Jonathan had either discharged his rifle accidently or fired a warning shot. Neil Marquis told police that his wife's wallet and keys were missing, but jewellery, money and other valuables were left untouched. The videos that Karen had rented that night, both Hollywood romantic comedies, had disappeared. Also missing from a bedroom cupboard were two *Playboy* magazines.

A warrant was quickly issued for Jonathan's arrest and the information relayed across Canada. Hamilton-Wentworth police were contacted and they faxed a copy of the police photograph of Jonathan that was taken when he was arrested for the attack on Alison. The RCMP released this photograph to the media. Every available police investigator in the Moncton area was assigned to assist in the search for the killer. Police interviewed an employee at a motel in the Fredricton area who reported that Jonathan had phoned ahead to reserve a room and arrived shortly after midnight, but then asked for cheaper accommodation and rejected what was offered him. He drove away in a westerly direction. He was apparently heading back toward Ontario.

Jonathan was next sighted in London, Ontario, 130 kilometres west of Hamilton. Subsequent investigations showed that he had been seen prior to that in several locations in the city. The first of these sightings was at 8:30 a.m. on August 13, when a woman noticed a man sleeping in a brown car parked in a shopping mall parking lot. She thought the car resembled one that had recently damaged her vehicle in a hit-and-run accident and for that reason made a note of the licence number, which turned out to be that of Jonathan's car.

That afternoon, Jonathan appeared at a downtown London bank, attempting to cash a 50-dollar cheque drawn on his account. After contacting his local branch, bank employees informed him that he only had enough funds deposited to cover a 36-dollar cheque. An assistant manager at the bank later supplied police with a detailed description of Jonathan. She said he was non-white, but not very black, slim, with curly black hair and a thin mustache, wearing an earring in his left ear and a sleeveless, teal blue undershirt. Jonathan presented no problems to the bank officer, who described him as very pleasant.

Jonathan spent the evening of August 13 at a bowling alley. Employees there would subsequently recall that he was friendly and talkative. He told them that he came from the east coast and that he was unfamiliar with ten-pin bowling. When someone noted that he looked as if he handled a bowling pin with ease, he admitted that he had done some bowling in Hamilton. A female employee watched him bowling and noticed his well-developed biceps. He seemed calm and relaxed as he chatted with her. He told her that he belonged to a church camp. Jonathan went into a games room at one point, where there were several video games, and he was described as "acting weird" and talking to the machines. He left the bowling alley at about 10 p.m. Employees particularly remembered his expressive and piercing eyes.

The incident that brought Jonathan to the attention of police was an attempted abduction of another young woman at about 1 a.m. on August 14. In the same neighbourhood as the bowling alley, Elizabeth, a 25-year-old woman, who was identified at the inquest as Ms M, was walking home from a friend's house. She had nearly reached her apartment building, when a boxy brown car pulled up in front of her. A man leaned out of the car window to ask her the way to Highway 401. He said he was lost and was trying to get to Brantford. He seemed confused and disoriented and asked Elizabeth to draw him a map, handing her a pen and a thin pad, which she later recognized was a cheque book. While she leaned over the hood of the car to draw a map on the pad, he got out of the car and hovered behind her.

Elizabeth turned toward him and realized that he was holding a rifle. She screamed in horror, but reacted by grabbing the gun. As he struggled to pull it away from her, he kept saying, "It's not a gun. It's not a gun." Elizabeth was certain that it was, and continued to hold onto it and scream as loudly as she could. Her building was well insulated for sound, however, and nobody responded. She used the gun as a lever to push the man away and ran the 30 metres to the front door of her building.

In her panic, she fumbled with her keys as she tried to open the door and her assailant caught up with her before she got inside. She could not see his gun and did not know whether he was hiding it from her or had left it by his car. He was pointing frantically at the pad on which she had been drawing the map. Elizabeth threw it at him and was relieved to find that he grabbed it and not her, giving her time to get inside and lock the door behind her.

She called the police and they responded within five minutes. She described her attacker as a fair-skinned black man wearing shorts, undershirt, running shoes and a cross-shaped earring dangling from one ear. From the description of the man and his car, the London police suspected that it might be Jonathan Yeo, about whom they had received an alert earlier in the day. Hamilton-Wentworth police were contacted and asked to fax a photograph of Jonathan. This was then shown to Elizabeth, who identified him as her attacker. A warning was broadcast to all police forces in the area.

Hamilton-Wentworth police again contacted Alison to warn

her to stay away from her apartment. Members of Jonathan's family were interviewed and urged to pass on any information they received about him. A stake-out was set up at the apartment building where his parents and his brother and sister-in-law lived. Niagara police were meanwhile watching his home. All this was organized quickly and efficiently by police forces that had not been interested in Jonathan less than a week earlier, when he was turned back from the border with a gun and what seemed to be a suicide note. Suddenly, nobody was worrying about the manpower shortage which had supposedly made it impractical for officers to collect evidence, to search for Jonathan's gun, to go to his house to arrest him on serious criminal charges or to issue a warrant for his arrest when he breached bail.

Having been informed by police that the net was closing in on Jonathan, his mother, Mae, listened on her police band radio and heard the reports and discussions of her son's last conscious moments. Jonathan was spotted driving along a street on the Hamilton Mountain near the southern city limits. Constable Myra James, driving alone in her cruiser, did a U-turn to fall in behind Jonathan's car. "We're going to go for a stroll," she reported over the radio, as Jonathan turned into the parking lot of a large shopping mall.

"Use extreme caution," said a radio dispatcher, informing the young constable that the suspect was considered suicidal and dangerous. The dispatcher warned that Jonathan may be in possession of a .22 calibre gun that had been used in a sexual assault and murder. Constable James continued to follow Jonathan's car, which was driving slowly at this point along a road, circling the shopping mall parking lot. He even stopped at the stop signs, perhaps still hoping that it was just a coincidence that there was a police car behind him.

Another cruiser arrived on the scene and fell in behind Constable James' vehicle. Jonathan was still driving very slowly, zigzagging in and out between parked cars, apparently trying to out-fox the police. This must have been a curious spectacle to shoppers who were out in numbers on the warm afternoon. One onlooker later compared Jonathan's little brown car to a frightened animal trying to escape from hunters.

Another car, driven by a sergeant, joined the chase, and he put on his siren and his flashing lights. He was worried that Jonathan was heading toward the most crowded section of the mall parking lot where buses were loading and unloading passengers. He considered ramming Jonathan's car but decided not to since police regulations had been recently changed to outlaw that method of stopping a suspect on the grounds that it was unsafe. Jonathan began to speed up, dangerously crossing into an oncoming lane of traffic and nearly going off the road as he rounded a curve. The police cars remained on his tail.

Suddenly the driver of one of the cruisers issued an urgent warning. "He's got the gun," said Constable Ian McElroy, who saw Jonathan holding the rifle in both hands, presumably steering the car with his knees. At this moment, Jonathan's car was enveloped in a cloud of dust as it veered to the right, mounted a muddy curb and then skidded across the road, colliding with a small grey car before sliding to a halt.

Jonathan was slumped forward against the steering wheel. He was bleeding profusely and appeared unconscious. But his rifle was pointing out the window and police had to assume that he still might pose a threat. The officers at the scene drew their weapons and carefully approached Jonathan's car. The occupants of the other car, a young mother and her baby, were shaken, but not injured. They were hustled out of the way.

The police told Jonathan to put down his weapon and leave the car, but there was no response. Slowly they approached the car and seized the gun. They handcuffed Jonathan's hands and feet. An ambulance was called and he was rushed to the Henderson General Hospital on the brow of the escarpment.

It was only after he had been medically examined that police realized Jonathan had shot himself in the head. The officers at the scene assumed that his injuries were caused by the impact of the crash. When he arrived at the hospital at 4:55 p.m. on August 14, 1991, he was bleeding heavily from the mouth and was not expected to live. Hospital staff did struggle for more than eight hours to save his life, however, and he was not finally pronounced dead until 3:20 a.m. He did not regain consciousness during the time he was in the hospital.

The evidence that police began to gather from the car confirmed Jonathan's guilt in the murder of Karen Marquis and the attack on the woman in London. Investigators found a cheque book, on the back of which was the map that Elizabeth had drawn to show him the way to Highway 401. The two video cassettes that Karen had rented were found in the car. Karen's green leather purse was also discovered, as was a torn portion of a CN pay stub, bearing her initials.

The car was messy and police found spent rifle cartridges and rounds of ammunition strewn among Number 7 cigarettes, fast food containers, empty Coke cans and paper coffee cups. Apparently, Jonathan had prepared himself for a trip, as the car contained clothes and two spare gas cans. He had also equipped himself with a supply of interlaced nylon ties, which are used in the electrical industry to hold cables, but are sometimes used by police as emergency handcuffs. Empty pill bottles were also found on the floor, but autopsy results did not show Jonathan to have had an unusually high level of anti-depressant drugs in his system.

The police also found the neatly folded note bearing Jonathan's expressions of intense self-loathing which he had been carrying when he tried to cross the border six days earlier. There was also a plastic shopping bag containing a collection of pornography, cut out pictures of women from magazines.

Blood stains found in the car and on Jonathan's clothing were examined by forensic experts. This analysis was not conclusive, but it was found that blood on Jonathan's jeans was similar to that of Karen Marquis's, while blood on his shoes belonged to the same blood group as that of Nina's.

After Nina's body was found, a firearms expert examined Jonathan's rifle in an attempt to determine whether it fired the bullets that killed Nina and Karen. The grooves on the inside of the barrel of a rifle put marks on a bullet which make it possible to determine whether the bullet was fired from that particular type of gun. Each gun also has its own scratches and imperfections, like individual fingerprints, which also get transferred onto the bullet. The firearms examiner was able to determine from the grooves that the bullets that killed both women were fired from a gun similar to Jonathan's. But it was not possible to detect the scratches on the bullets because they were too disfigured from impact with the bones in the victims' skulls. The examiner also found that the bullets were of a similar type to those found in Jonathan's car.

Jonathan's rifle was at least 30 years old. The examiner noted that it required considerably less pressure to pull the trigger than a newer model, but that it was not prone to accidental discharge. The rifle was manufactured before a law was introduced requiring that all such guns carry serial numbers.

At the time that the rifle was made, it was not necessary to have a licence to own such a gun. A subsequent law made it necessary for anyone buying a rifle to get a firearms acquisition certificate. This covers rifles and shotguns which are used primarily for hunting. People wishing to purchase a handgun, which is considered a restricted weapon, must apply for a special permit. Any adult who is not mentally ill and has no record for violent crime can obtain a firearms acquisition certificate fairly easily. It remains in effect for ten years and it entitles the person to own an unlimited number of guns. There is no central registry of FACs and no easy way for authorities to match the certificate with the serial numbers of the guns.

Jonathan would not have been required to have an FAC at all if his gun was purchased before the FACs were introduced. Ammunition for such guns is readily available over the counter at any hardware store. No certificate is required to purchase ammunition.

In all Jonathan's violent episodes he appeared to be extremely volatile, but also at times ambivalent about following through with his worst intentions. When he brandished a knife in his attacks, many victims were able to fend him off long enough to get away or to cause him to have second thoughts. He may well not have killed anyone if he had not armed himself with a gun that required a mere two pounds of force to pull the trigger. Stricter gun laws would not necessarily have stopped him from carrying a weapon if he was determined to do so. Nor would bail conditions prohibiting the possession of a firearm. But the absence of such restrictions certainly made it easier for Jonathan to kill.

The police investigation of the Karen Marquis murder concluded with Jonathan's death. The investigating officer was satisfied that the evidence overwhelmingly showed that Jonathan Yeo was the perpetrator. The investigators in Burlington recognized that much of their evidence was circumstantial, but deemed it "totally inconsistent with any other rational conclusion" than that Jonathan shot and killed Nina behind the racquet club.

▼

Jonathan's funeral was a small, private affair. His family made sure that the media were not aware of it until afterward. Jonathan's mother, Mae, subsequently told a newspaper reporter, "No one else can hurt him now. Whatever demons he had are gone now." His father, Raymond, collapsed during the ceremony and had to be taken home before it was over. The couple has since moved from Hamilton to a nearby city in order to avoid further notoriety. Mae said after the funeral, "Everyone knows us here and I can't walk out the door."

The saddest comment from Jonathan's family about his death came nearly a year later at the coroner's inquest. His brother, James, and sister-in-law, Laura, approached Priscilla to offer their condolences. James told her that he was sorry for her loss. Priscilla told them that she was sorry for the Yeo family's loss. Laura responded by saying, "I feel like we didn't lose anything worth keeping."

Part Four
A COMMUNITY SEEKS JUSTICE

eleven

EVIDENCE
AT THE INQUEST

▼

T HE FULL ENORMITY OF the errors which led to Nina's murder
was not exposed until April 1992, when a coroner's inquest
began hearing evidence. This was an inquest into Jonathan's death.
But all the circumstances that led to his crimes — and allowed him
to get away with them — were considered in 44 days of hearings,
during which 108 witnesses were called and more than 300 items of
evidence were examined.

Soon after he died, some startling details of how Jonathan's case
was mismanaged were exposed in the media. Questions were raised
about his release on bail without any prohibition against carrying a
weapon. Strong criticisms were voiced concerning the decision by
Canadian border officials not to detain him after he tried to enter
the United States with a rifle.

At that stage, however, no one realized how many people had
blundered or how many systems had failed. Government officials
were reluctant even to investigate. When the media or the de
Villiers family posed questions, people in authority responded with
evasions and misinformation. No one was prepared to accept
responsibility for having allowed an armed and dangerous man to
remain free.

When Ontario's chief coroner James Young first announced in
the fall of 1991 that he would conduct a major inquest into

Jonathan's death, Priscilla found it difficult to believe that it would be anything other than a cosmetic exercise. She was already disillusioned with the justice system, which had repeatedly frustrated all her attempts to learn more about why her daughter died.

Priscilla had little faith that an inquest would tackle the really tough questions about how the system failed her daughter. Evidence for coroner's inquests is usually gathered by the police and presented in court by a coroner's counsel, a lawyer appointed to represent the coroner. In most cases, the coroner's counsel is a Crown attorney, whose normal duties involve prosecuting criminal cases.

A senior Crown attorney visited Priscilla to give his personal assurance that all her questions would be raised at the inquest. She told him that she could not trust the Crown to conduct an unbiased investigation or to represent her interests in any way. The best way of ensuring that the right questions were raised at the inquest was for Priscilla to ask her own questions.

The law provides for people who have a direct interest in the proceedings at a coroner's inquest to seek "standing" at the hearing, so that they or their lawyers can question witnesses, call evidence and make submissions. Coroners invariably grant standing to the family of the deceased person and to any individuals or institutions who may have played a role in the circumstances that led to the death. They often deny standing to groups or individuals with a less direct interest in the outcome of the hearing. Priscilla was angry when a representative of the coroner's office warned her that her request would not necessarily be granted. "If I don't deserve standing, who does?" she asked, only to be told that it would be unusual for her to be given standing since this was an inquest into the death of Jonathan Yeo, not Nina.

A team of Ontario Provincial Police officers was charged with responsibility for gathering evidence and the chief coroner decided to appoint a defence lawyer rather than a Crown attorney as his counsel. This decision addressed Priscilla's concern that a Crown attorney could not be expected to conduct an unbiased investigation of his or her own colleagues.

Nevertheless, Priscilla was still deeply distrustful of the process and remained determined to seek standing. She decided that she would try to do without a lawyer, at least to begin with, since lawyers whom she contacted quoted fees ranging from 150 dollars to 400 dollars per hour.

There were ten lawyers in the courtroom when Priscilla appeared before the Coroner to ask for standing. She knew that she had little knowledge of the law and realized that emotionally she was still not in a state to deal calmly and objectively with the evidence that would emerge at the inquest. She was all the more determined to go ahead with her application, however, when she observed that the lawyers, the coroner, the police investigators — in fact, everyone connected with the court, with the exception of a stenographer — were all men. Yet this was a case involving male violence against women. Nearly all the people involved in the investigation of Jonathan were male and the investigation had been severely compromised by gross insensitivity to female victims. It was obvious that there needed to be a female voice in the courtroom, someone to speak for the women who had died and the others who had been hurt.

The purpose of a coroner's inquest is to determine the cause of death and shed light on the circumstances in which the death occurred. It is not a forum for apportioning blame, but for making recommendations that could save other lives. Priscilla made it clear that she was not interested in pointing fingers at anyone. It was too late for that. But she was determined that lessons should be learned and that steps be taken to ensure that other young women would be better protected than Nina had been.

Priscilla was granted standing, along with lawyers representing Sheila Yeo, the Ontario attorney-general's ministry, Canada Customs and the Federal Immigration Department, Ontario

Correctional Services, the Niagara and Hamilton-Wentworth Regional Police, the defence lawyer who represented Jonathan at the bail hearing and all the doctors who treated or assessed him in various psychiatric hospitals. There were obviously many individuals and institutions who felt they might need to protect their interests in light of the evidence that might emerge.

About a month before the inquest began, each of the persons with standing was given a large box containing 12 volumes of briefs. These were the statements and documents collected by the police officers investigating on behalf of the coroner. For several weeks, Rocco and Priscilla spent their evenings and a large part of their nights poring over these documents, underlining, making notes and queries. They were made aware for the first time of the inadequacies in the police investigations of Jonathan and of all the ways in which a careless, inefficient and insensitive system had failed a succession of female victims whose stories were never told in a court of law. Priscilla furiously studied the law and prepared to represent the victims whom the system had failed to protect.

When the five-person coroner's jury was appointed, Priscilla was relieved to find that it included three women. However, she and her friends decided to make sure that there were a number of women attending the hearing every day. They felt that it was important to remind the male representatives of the legal system that members of the community — and especially women in the community — were watching and listening very carefully.

The inquest began on April 13, 1992, in a huge makeshift courtroom which previously housed the registry office on the ground floor of the Hamilton-Wentworth Court House. Priscilla and the 11 lawyers who attended the first day of the hearing sat behind three rows of tables facing the coroner, Dr. Young, the police officers who were assisting him, the court reporter and a large pile of documents and exhibits. The acoustics in the cavernous courtroom were so bad that people sitting in the body of the court were constantly leaning forward in their seats and straining to hear. The lawyers and witnesses struggled with a sound system that frequently failed to pick up what was being said or, conversely, shook the room with a fierce screech of feedback. Beside Dr. Young, a board had been erected bearing the coroner's motto: "From the death of one, we may learn to help lengthen the lives of many."

Ted Minden, the coroner's counsel, was a meticulously thorough man who was evidently determined to leave no stone unturned. He was no doubt aware that Priscilla and others were skeptical about the justice system's ability to investigate itself. He had therefore planned to explore every possible avenue of evidence during the three to four months that had been set aside for the hearing. The evidence was divided up into nine phases. The inquest would begin by examining its prime focus, Jonathan's death and those of his victims. Then it would consider in turn Jonathan's earlier violent acts against women, the sexual assault that led to criminal charges, the bail hearing, his dealings with psychiatrists and the border incident. The last two phases would be the evidence about Jonathan's background and family life, followed by expert witnesses, who would provide their analysis of some of the issues raised.

Once the hearing got under way, Priscilla was pleasantly surprised to find that she was treated very respectfully by the lawyers. However, it was extremely difficult for her to deal, once again, with the details surrounding her daughter's death and to hear them coolly presented and analysed as cold, hard pieces of evidence.

The jury was asked to confirm the conclusions of the police investigations which found that Jonathan had murdered Nina and Karen. No other interpretation of the evidence was possible, particularly in the light of a series of forensic tests that were completed just before the inquest began. There was never any doubt that Jonathan murdered Karen, since his fingerprint was found at the scene. The Halton Regional Police were convinced, on the basis of circumstantial evidence, that he also killed Nina. But the Ontario Provincial Police, the force responsible for policing the area where the body was found, had raised doubts and suggested that DNA tests be completed in order to prove beyond doubt that Jonathan was Nina's murderer.

DNA, an abbreviation for deoxyribonucleic acid, is a genetic code contained in chromosomes within the nucleus of every human cell. Each person has an identical DNA pattern in every cell of his or her body and there is generally less than a one-in-a-million chance that any two people would have the same DNA patterns, unless they are identical twin brothers or sisters. Thus, it is possible for scientists to use DNA as a genetic fingerprint which will identify the source of any sample containing a human cell. This is a slow process as it involves exposing a series of samples to x-ray films for long periods of time. The purpose of the tests conducted at the forensic lab in Toronto was to determine whether it was Nina's blood that had been found in Jonathan's car.

Unfortunately Nina's body was so badly decomposed that it was not possible to take a sample that could be compared with the blood stains. Since DNA patterns are made up of a series of paired characteristics, each of which is inherited from one parent, Nina's parents were asked to supply the forensic laboratory with samples of their own blood. Scientists were then able to compare Rocco and Priscilla's DNA patterns with cell samples taken from the blood stains in Jonathan's car. From this comparison they concluded that the blood in the car came from a female child of Rocco and Priscilla de Villiers.

It was especially difficult for Priscilla to deal with this and other evidence about her daughter's murder presented at the inquest. She was under the constant scrutiny of the media, who crowded into the courtroom during the first few days, until the majority of them got bored with the slow pace of the proceedings. While television crews and still photographers waited to get pictures of her outside, reporters inside the courtroom noted carefully how she reacted to the more dramatic or emotionally charged moments in the proceedings. Priscilla was surprised to see one newspaper column which gave a sentimental description of how she had flinched and looked away when Jonathan's gun was produced in court. She was not aware of making such a response and had no idea that the columnist was even in the court, let alone watching and interpreting her every move.

The tables in front of the coroner's bench were cluttered with exhibits during the first two stages of the inquest. The scattered remnants found in the wake of three violent deaths lay spread out on the table a few feet away from Priscilla: Jonathan's gun; the bullet fragments found lodged in his own and his victims' skulls; Nina's headband; Jonathan's bloodstained shoes; Karen's purse; the two light-hearted videos found in Jonathan's car that Karen had planned to watch on the night she died; the bag of clothes that Nina had purchased before she went to the tennis club; the note in which Jonathan described himself as "Mr. Dirt."

Then there were the live victims: the testimonies of the women whom Jonathan terrorized, but did not kill. It was difficult not to connect their harrowing stories with what might have happened to Nina and Karen in their last moments.

Priscilla sat stoically through most of the testimony, occasionally asking the victims questions about what might have encouraged them to come forward sooner. The evidence of Jonathan's early victims was an eloquent indictment of the legal system's insensitivity. Jonathan's first victim, Sandra, never disclosed what happened, because she was afraid that she would again be victimized by the system and not believed. After all, her mother, Carol, had pressed charges and taken her case to court, where she was confronted with disbelief. When Janet's father told police that his daughter was being harassed and threatened, he was informed that the police could do nothing unless Janet had been physically harmed. Lindsey, whom Jonathan attacked with a knife, could not persuade police to take her case seriously enough to lay charges.

It was a vicious circle in which the law failed female victims and women lost confidence in the law, afraid to seek even the limited protection that it seemed to offer. As a consequence, Jonathan went on attacking women for more than a decade without ever being brought to account. There was no way of telling how many more women he had hurt, besides those who came forward at the inquest. One could see in the women's accounts of these attacks that Jonathan was getting gradually bolder and more unstable. For his own good, as well as that of all his potential victims, he needed to be stopped before it was too late.

His family could have stopped him, but their choice was to try to protect him from a penal system in which they had no confidence. Jonathan's mother-in-law, Nancy, testified that she did not believe that he would get the help he needed if he went to prison. She had worked with prisoners for many years and was speaking from experience. Psychiatric and counselling services in the correctional system are notoriously impoverished and it is true that few prisoners obtain the help they need.

However, Nancy was not helping Jonathan by allowing him to evade the consequences of his actions. Psychiatrists subsequently agreed that he was suffering from a personality disorder, which could only be treated if he recognized the need to change his antisocial behaviour. His family's reactions led him to believe that he was not responsible for his actions and that his behaviour was beyond his control.

The evidence of Yvonne, Sheila Yeo's 24-year-old cousin, whom Jonathan raped, was particularly troubling. It illustrated all the fundamental reasons why Jonathan's violence was never stopped — his victim's reluctance to come forward, her concerns about police insensitivity and the family's practice of standing by in the face of his crimes.

Priscilla lost her composure when she heard Yvonne's testimony and that of Nancy, who was present while her niece deliberated whether to lay charges against her son-in-law. Horrified to hear that the young woman was left alone with Sheila and Jonathan soon after the assault, Priscilla began her cross-examination of Yvonne's mother by saying, "For two days, we have heard endlessly about the effect on the family, Sheila and her children. I've hardly heard one word about the victim and this concerns me a lot. Were you alone with your daughter when she came back from the medical centre?"

"I can't remember that I was," the mother replied.

"Did you ever discuss what she felt before she went to the farm?"

"I think we tried to reassure her that we were concerned for her, supporting her and loving her," said the mother, whose testimony was punctuated with long pauses.

Priscilla went on to say, "As a mother, you must feel huge pain. It concerns me that, when your daughter said she felt safe with you and your sister, you left her to face Jonathan and Sheila. Did you ask her if she felt comfortable?"

Yvonne's mother replied, "I can't remember that we did."

"I know this may seem hurtful. But I feel very strongly that the victim was forgotten," said Priscilla.

This was one of the worst moments of the inquest for Priscilla. She could see very plainly the impossible dilemma that was faced by this young woman, trapped in what seemed from the outside to be a dangerously unhealthy family dynamic. Priscilla was so distraught that one of the lawyers suggested that he ask the coroner to adjourn the hearing. But Priscilla wanted to continue. She was more convinced than ever that she had a crucial role to play. It seemed clear to her that the judicial system had to be made more sensitive and accessible to victims, so that women who are beaten or abused by family members need not feel isolated and trapped.

Yvonne might have felt more confident about laying charges if she had received encouragement from the counsellor from the Hamilton Sexual Assault Centre, who saw her at the hospital. But, instead, the counsellor had painted a bleak picture of the justice system, suggesting that Yvonne could face intimidation from police and aggressive cross-examination in court. She also intimated that the courts usually set rapists free and that police provide little protection. Instead of promising on-going counselling and support in negotiating the legal system, the counsellor gave Yvonne a handful of pamphlets and her card, saying that she could call her if she wished. Yvonne felt shy about making such a phone call and did not contact the Sexual Assault Centre. She later told the court at the inquest that she would have gladly gone for counselling, if an appointment had been set up for her.

There may well have been some truth in the counsellor's harsh description of the system's treatment of sexual assault victims. But when the counsellor testified at the inquest, she cited statistics for which she was able to supply no source or verification. She told the court that rape is not an indictable offence and that most rapists are given sentences of less than two years, because the courts want to protect them by not giving them criminal records. She also confused the very simple legal term "charged" (being accused of an offence) with "convicted" (being found guilty). The lawyers at the inquest rolled their eyes at these comments, which were not only untrue, but displayed a total ignorance of the law.

Nevertheless, one could easily understand the sexual assault counsellor's distrust of police after hearing the evidence of Alison and the police constable who dealt with her after her ordeal. Constable Kenneth Wilson explained that he did not believe Alison's story of being held hostage and sexually assaulted by an armed man because she did not seem hysterical. This prompted Priscilla to begin her cross-examination by saying, "If I told you that in nine months of dealing with two police forces, only two policemen have ever seen me shed a tear, would you say that I have no grief?"

"No," the police officer replied in a chastened tone. He acknowledged that he had been wrong, but added that previous experience of other cases where women had made false allegations had made him skeptical.

Later, when expert witnesses were called, the inquest learned that Constable Wilson, like most other police officers, probably received very little training. In Ontario, new recruits are sent on a 47-day training course before going out on the streets. For many police officers, that may be all the training they ever receive in their careers, apart from the odd weekend workshop or in-house session.

An expert testified that Wilson's response to Alison could have been used in a course as an object lesson in how *not* to deal with a sexual assault complainant. The expert suggested that someone with his lack of training and his attitudes should not be assigned to deal with cases of alleged sexual assault, which should be handled by teams of specially trained officers, hand-picked for the task. After the inquest, the Hamilton-Wentworth Regional Police established sexual assault teams to deal with such cases in future.

The inquest exposed a host of other problems involving police procedures and organization. One constant theme was lack of communication between various police forces, which have different levels of technological sophistication and few standardized common procedures for keeping records or sharing information. While Jonathan was committing a murder in New Brunswick, police were on the look-out for him in Niagara and Hamilton-Wentworth. Meanwhile an alert had been issued about Nina's disappearance, but it was only circulated to forces in southern Ontario. The evidence painted an unsettling picture of police forces as ill-equipped and inefficient bureaucracies that had not yet mastered modern technologies for handling and sharing information.

Detective Brian Leng, a senior investigator, who said he was too busy to leave the office to make an arrest or obtain a search warrant to look for a weapon, had been laboriously typing his own reports with two fingers. The police station from which he worked did not have a fax machine and the courier service took more than two days to deliver a vital report from the central station — a 15-minute drive away. The inquest heard that the mistakes made in Jonathan's case had already prompted Hamilton-Wentworth Regional Police to create new computerized forms, which would ensure that reports were prepared correctly for bail court. Several months passed, however, before all the computers were set up to handle these forms and many officers did not use them because they were intimidated by computers.

Leng acknowledged that he should have been particularly conscious of the need to ensure that a dangerous man not have access to a gun while out on bail, since other officers had made a similar mistake a few months earlier with equally tragic consequences. In February 1991, 33-year-old George Lovie was arrested and charged with forcible confinement and sexual assault with a weapon in connection with a brutal attack on his former girlfriend. He held the woman at knife point for several hours and at one point showed her some bullets and a permit for a gun, saying that he intended to kill her because she had decided to end their relationship. Lovie had not been in any trouble with the law during the previous ten years and police officers believed that he should be granted bail. They followed a procedure which was then common, but has since been curtailed, of consenting to his release before a justice of the peace at the police station without involving a Crown attorney. There was no condition prohibiting Lovie from possessing a firearm.

Before Lovie was released, a police officer was informed that there was no record of Lovie obtaining a firearms acquisition certificate. Without a certificate, the officer did not believe that Lovie could carry out his threat of obtaining a gun. But on March 21, 1991, Lovie appeared with a knife and a gun at his former girlfriend's house. He chased her to the neighbouring home of her parents, where he was confronted by her mother whom he fatally shot and then by her father whom he stabbed to death.

Leng was one of the officers called upon to assist in the arrest. When Lovie was brought into custody and searched, a firearms acquisition certificate was found in his wallet. The investigating officer again phoned the records office and was told that no such certificate had been issued. It turned out that someone had misplaced the file.

It is difficult to understand how a similar mistake could have been made less than two months later in a case that also involved forcible confinement, sexual assault, a knife, bullets and a gun. Leng acknowledged in his testimony that he should have searched for Jonathan's gun and that he forgot to recommend that he be prohibited from possessing a firearm while on bail. He explained that such oversights occurred because the investigation had been protracted over a long period of time. He had been very busy and frequently distracted with other matters that demanded his immediate attention.

While Detective Leng was testifying, Priscilla decided she needed to enlist the services of a lawyer. Leng frequently disputed the suggestions that were made to him during painstaking examination and cross-examinations. He said that "in the real world" the problems are more complex than implied in questions that were being put with the benefit of "twenty-twenty hindsight." Priscilla felt that he was evading the issues. She was afraid that the police and the Crown attorneys whose evidence was to follow would be able to wriggle off the hook. She did not feel that she had the skills required to pin them down in the cross-examination process.

Priscilla hired Mark Sandler, an experienced defence lawyer who previously worked for several years as a Crown attorney. Although Sandler was a lawyer who could command very high fees, he was concerned enough about the issues involved that he agreed to work at the reduced rate that lawyers are paid for legal aid work.

Sandler's presence changed the tenor of the hearing. An affable, mild-mannered man outside the courtroom, he could be ferocious and unrelenting in cross-examination. He badgered police officers, Crown attorneys and civil servants until they acknowledged their mistakes and identified the failings of the systems for which they were responsible.

Priscilla found it a huge relief to be represented by a lawyer. It had been increasingly difficult to maintain her composure at the hearing. Even though the lawyers present represented different interests, they developed the kind of camaraderie that usually emerges during the course of a long case. As they became more relaxed with one another, they would tend to share jokes and talk glibly about tactics or strategies. While Priscilla understood that this was normal, she found it difficult to accept that some of the lawyers could approach the circumstances of her daughter's death as if it were a game. Now that she had a lawyer acting on her behalf, she was more able to relax with the confidence that her interests were being ably represented.

The inquest moved on to probe the mistakes and shortcomings that led to Jonathan being released on bail without being prohibited from possessing a firearm. Michael Fox, the inexperienced prosecutor in the bail hearing, was questioned at length about the decisions he had made in the intensely pressured setting of an overcrowded court. The inquest was told that 15 prosecutors in the Hamilton-Wentworth Crown attorney's office handle a total of 25,000 criminal cases a year. Each of them has to appear in court every day in order to staff 15 courtrooms, in some of which as many as 40 cases are heard and 150 more remanded. The inquest heard that it is a rule of thumb in the legal profession that ten hours of preparation should be devoted to every hour in court, but that Crown prosecutors can devote very little time to preparation since they spend most of their working days in court. Fox testified that he spent only a few minutes looking at the brief in preparation for Jonathan's bail hearing and did not even have time to read all the material.

While this explained what had happened, there was little doubt that a properly prepared and skilful prosecutor could have made a powerful case for keeping Jonathan in custody. It was not because the bail laws were too liberal that Jonathan went free. Nor was it because the justice of the peace was ill-trained and lacked a good understanding of the law, although the inquest did indeed find that the training of justices of the peace is woefully inadequate. Jonathan was released because the Crown failed to fashion all the available information and arguments into a compelling case. One can fault the justice of the peace for not imposing a firearms restriction, but she may well have done so if the Crown or the police had remembered to ask for one.

David Carr, the Hamilton-Wentworth Crown attorney, was questioned at length about the apparent shortcomings of his office, which allowed a young prosecutor to handle such a serious case without any preparation. Who had trained him? Who was monitoring his performance? Why did the prosecutor not have any advance notice of a case which had been remanded several times already? Why was the case not flagged as one meriting special attention and assigned to a senior Crown? Why could sexual assault cases not be assigned immediately to a prosecutor with special training and expertise in that area?

These and similar questions were vigorously pursued, but Carr was not prepared to admit that his office was at fault. He said that he had confidence in his staff to do the best they could with the resources available. Carr maintained that Michael Fox was well aware that he could have done a better job with the bail hearing and would learn from his mistakes. He explained that he had an "open door" policy in his office and that Fox knew that he could consult with him at any time about a case if he needed to. Some changes had been implemented already, he said, to allow more time for preparation of bail cases. It was simply not possible from an administrative point of view to assign cases to individual prosecutors at such an early stage.

The Crown attorney estimated that the charges arising from Jonathan's attack on Alison would probably have resulted in a prison term of three or four years. He said he would have asked a judge to impose a five- or six-year sentence if he was able to call evidence to suggest that Jonathan was dangerous to women. A member of the coroner's jury asked Carr why he would not ask for a much longer sentence. Carr explained that the courts would ignore such a submission. He said 14 years was the maximum sentence for the offences with which Jonathan was charged, but the maximum penalty is reserved for the worst offender and the worst set of aggravating circumstances. Jonathan did not qualify for that, said Carr, who agreed, however, when a juror observed, "Today he does."

Carr's boss James Treleaven, the regional director of Crown attorneys, identified 14 changes that needed to be made in the operation of the Crown attorney's office and expressed concern that bail hearings were still not being conducted properly. As a resident of Burlington with a teenaged daughter, Treleaven testified that he was disturbed personally as well as professionally when he heard of Nina's death. He said that he had rarely seen a more serious case than the one that brought Jonathan to court in June 1991. There was no doubt in his mind that Jonathan should have been detained, he said, asserting that his staff should be prepared to admit their mistakes and learn from them. Many of the changes that he suggested were simple procedural matters. "It's not rocket science," he said. Later Treleaven softened the impact of these forthright comments by saying in cross-examination that he had not intended to be critical of Carr and his staff.

It was distressing to learn from extensive psychiatric evidence that mental health professionals feel helpless when confronted with someone like Jonathan. His family was looking for a miraculous cure. Police and Crown lawyers thought that psychiatrists would be able to detain him if he proved to be dangerous. But psychiatrists were unable to help him or hold him. They admitted that they do not have the answers to the kind of personality and behavioural problems that Jonathan presented. The behavioural psychology programs that might be able to help dangerously disturbed individuals such as Jonathan Yeo are inadequately funded and seldom available. As for research into better treatment methods, one doctor lamented that there is far more money available for the study of tooth decay.

While psychiatrists could clearly see that Jonathan was dangerous, it was not their mandate to lock up somebody they believed they could not treat. Psychiatrists pointed out that they are not gatekeepers and their job is to heal, not to protect the public. Protection is the job of the police and the courts. Since Jonathan had not made any direct threat, they could not even warn anyone about their concerns. Their professional guidelines allowed them to waive the rules of medical confidentiality only in cases where they believed that a specific crime was going to be committed. To disclose information in other circumstances undermines the basic trust that must exist between doctor and patient.

The psychiatrists, who described Jonathan as a time bomb, saw him as just one of many dangerous individuals and volatile people walking the streets. One doctor, whose entire practice involves patients in trouble with the law, explained that if he were required to detain all the dangerous individuals whom he saw, he would never be able to let anyone leave his office. An expert psychiatric witness told the court, "Society doesn't have any method of dealing with someone who *might* do something. We're surrounded by these people. Some of them don't get into trouble and some of them do."

The same expert was asked what a psychiatrist could do if a patient or his family discusses previous acts of violence of which the police and the courts were not aware. This was a key issue in Jonathan's case, since hospital records, to which the police had no access, contained information about his history of violence against women. The expert replied, "I doubt if you can do anything. If you went to the Crown attorney, you wouldn't have any proof other than the patient's statements."

According to the statements made by the experts, there was nothing that psychiatrists could do to stop Jonathan. However, he could have been stopped when he tried to cross the Canada–United States border. Unfortunately none of the people involved realized that he or she had the power.

The most impressive witness to testify at the inquest was Hugh O'Hear, the United States immigration officer. He was the one person who correctly assessed the danger that Jonathan posed. He saw that this threat should be treated as a priority. Setting aside his other pressing duties at a very busy time, he did what he could to persuade Canadian officials to take action.

A legal expert testified that police had the power to arrest Jonathan for attempting to breach his bail under two different sections of the criminal code. But none of the police officers on the Canadian side of the border who talked to O'Hear that evening was aware of these laws. In fact, when O'Hear told them that they must have such powers, they informed him that he was mistaken. The coroner's counsel, Ted Minden, observed, "What happened at the Whirlpool Bridge defies any rational explanation."

If the circumstances were not so bleak, one could derive some humour from the antics of the Canadian border guards who chose to hide in their booths and speed Jonathan on his way without asking him any questions that might upset him. It seemed like a parody of a bureaucracy gone mad when witnesses explained that Jonathan had left Canada according to the immigration officials, but not in the eyes of the customs officers.

"Can members of the community not count on our officials whom we rely on to protect us to use common sense?" asked Minden. He suggested that too many of the officials involved in

Jonathan's case were "going through the motions like the factory workers in a Charlie Chaplin film."

Police, Crown attorneys, border guards and other civil servants all blamed the law and the system for the circumstances that led to Nina's death. But the inquest reached a different conclusion. It appeared that safeguards did exist in the system. There were laws available that could have been applied to put Jonathan behind bars and take his gun away before he became out of control. These laws were not used because of the failures of individuals whom Priscilla's lawyer Mark Sandler characterized as "prosecutors who didn't prosecute, police who didn't police and counsellors who didn't counsel."

Sandler asked, on Priscilla's behalf, for recommendations that would make officials more accountable to the public. Describing Priscilla as "the most courageous, compassionate, decent woman I know," Sandler went on to say, "She doesn't seek vengeance. She seeks change. She is not interested in sympathy or remorse from the system — just competence."

In his final submission, Minden told the coroner's jury, "The evidence is clear that Jonathan Yeo did not slip through the cracks of the system. He slipped through the hands of people in the system. That is the sad truth."

twelve

THE JURY'S
RECOMMENDATIONS

▼

THE DEATHS OF Nina, Karen and Jonathan might have been prevented if it were not for a long series of mistakes that the inquest exposed. The first of these mistakes occurred as early as 1979, when someone forgot to take Jonathan's fingerprints after he had been charged with assault. The errors continued right up until the evening Jonathan was waved through the Canadian border station with a loaded rifle in the back of his car.

The mistakes that led to Nina's death combined with a series of unfortunate coincidences. As one considers all the circumstances, it is difficult to distinguish between error and chance. Nina made a mistake about the time of her tennis tournament. No one would dream of suggesting that any blame lay in that oversight. In hindsight, it was evidently a mistake for Nina to have gone jogging at dusk. Yet it should not have been a mistake, as she and all other women should have the right to walk or run anywhere at any time and remain unmolested. It would not have been a mistake, were it not for a random encounter with an armed man who was at large by virtue of the grievous errors that others had made.

Some mistakes arose from ignorance and others from carelessness. Many were attributable to overwork, lack of resources and education and inefficiently designed systems. A few of the most fatal errors were just plain dumb. People overlooked the obvious and forgot to follow basic procedures which training and experience should have made second nature to them.

Dr. Young, the coroner, commented at the end of the inquest, "As life gets more complex, sometimes the painfully obvious gets lost. The story of how the obvious is overlooked is unfortunately what keeps us in business."

It is difficult to see how one can always guard against human error, especially in the criminal justice system where people from different professions work together through a complex network of agencies, jurisdictions, institutions and bureaucracies. Such a system is bound to make mistakes when it deals continually with the most unpredictable and poorly understood aspects of human nature. It is inevitable that there will be cracks through which dangerous and volatile people are likely to fall.

Nevertheless, the system cannot afford to be tolerant of its own shortcomings. The fact that there are cracks must not be allowed to become an excuse for complacency. There may well be many deaths that cannot be prevented, but that is not a reason to overlook those that could and should have been prevented.

That is what Ted Minden, the coroner's counsel, told the coroner's jury at the inquest. He asked the jurors to find that the crimes which were committed were preventable. Suggesting that they recommend sweeping changes, he urged the jurors, "Make people in the system accountable to others. Ensure that those charged with the responsibility and trust of protecting the public are the right people to carry out that trust. Ensure that they never forget the case of Jonathan Yeo."

The jury made 137 recommendations. An inquest is not supposed to apportion blame, but it was obvious that the jurors had a clear idea where much of the fault lay. More than a third of the recommendations were directed at the Hamilton-Wentworth Regional Police, while another substantial proportion involved the procedures of the regional Crown attorney's office. At the same time, however, the recommendations continually suggested that public officials everywhere should examine their own procedures and attitudes. There were universal lessons to be learned from the particular mistakes.

Most of the jury's proposals related to quite specific problems, failings and oversights which the inquest had identified. They were practical, detailed recommendations which had been suggested by Minden and agreed to by all the other lawyers present. They proposed that training programs be set up and checklists prepared for people to follow while carrying out their everyday duties. Many of these proposed programs and lists covered very basic procedures, such as remembering to look for weapons while arresting someone for a violent crime or making sure that Crown attorneys read their briefs before conducting a bail hearing.

Besides safeguarding against individual mistakes, the recommendations were designed to ensure that the system did not allow errors to remain unchecked and be repeated. By calling for written directives, checklists and procedural rules, the jury tried to ensure that it no longer be possible for anyone in the bureaucracy to pass the buck. Once the recommendations were implemented, it should become clear precisely what each individual was supposed to do. It should also be possible to find out whether people were being properly instructed and well supervised.

The recommendations encouraged the police and Crown attorney's office to set priorities and attempt to distinguish cases like Jonathan's that require special attention from routine cases that make up the bulk of their workload. Procedures were proposed for identifying all cases involving sexual violence and weapons and putting them in the hands of specially trained investigators and prosecutors. The jury proposed that investigators be instructed to show sensitivity and compassion towards victims, check accused people's backgrounds, find out about their mental state and obtain search warrants to look for weapons. Prosecutors were urged to talk to victims and study all the court documents in advance of the bail hearing. Checklists were suggested as a means of reminding Crown attorneys of the issues that they should canvas and the arguments that they might make in opposing bail or seeking strict conditions of release.

Many of the measures that were recommended were simple and obvious procedures that should have been in place long before. While cross-examining witnesses during the inquest, Mark Sandler, the de Villiers' lawyer, made suggestions to the police and the local Crown's office about basic procedures that he believed should be followed. When a senior police officer agreed wholeheartedly with many of his proposals, Sandler was gratified, but a little alarmed. He said, "Why are Sandler and Minden telling the Hamilton police how to do their job? It's very disturbing that they're discovering how to be a police force sitting here in this room."

Members of the jury were obviously disturbed by what they heard. So much so, that the jury's final 11 recommendations proposed far-reaching changes in government policy and in law. The first of these was prefaced by the comment: "We the jury, representing the people of Ontario, are losing faith in our justice system due to the lack of accountability by our public officials. Our law enforcement agencies seem unable to stop the proliferation of crimes in the streets and homes of our communities, particularly violent criminal offences with weapons."

The jury went on to recommend establishing a provincial commission with representation from all sectors of society to study how to make officials in the justice system more accountable for the protection, security and safety of the people. The jurors stated that they had tried to stress accountability in their general recommendations. Accountability had been a key concept that was emphasized by Priscilla and her lawyer throughout the inquest.

A charter of victims' rights was proposed by the jury in order to prevent victims from being re-victimized by the system. The jury suggested that such a charter would guarantee the rights of victims be protected, supported with emotional counselling, informed of the progress of the investigation or prosecution and notified if the perpetrator was to be released from custody.

Another recommendation was for a central registry of violent sexual assaults. This would be a confidential information resource shared by law enforcement agencies. It would collect information on all occurrences involving sexual violence or the use of a weapon in a sexual offence. Incidents such as Jonathan's earlier assaults, which did not result in criminal charges, could be recorded in such a data base. The jury's idea was that this might help identify serial rapists or other dangerous offenders by making the kind of connections that were woefully lacking in Jonathan's case.

The jury also recommended a firearms registry, which would keep track of all firearms and gun licences. People applying for a firearms acquisition licence would have their photos taken and would have to register the serial number of each gun they owned or acquired. Anyone wishing to purchase a gun would have to wait a week, while authorities made sure that everything was in order.

In what ought to have been a statement of the obvious, the jury noted that it is imperative that justices of the peace presiding over bail hearings should be competent to conduct them. Expert testimony at the inquest had suggested that many justices of the peace are not, in fact, properly trained or knowledgeable of the law. The jury recommended that justices of the peace be involved in mandatory training and assessment. The recommendation proposed that justices be provided with a comprehensive and easy-to-read manual on bail hearings, including a checklist of items to be considered when setting conditions for release. Another proposed that judges rather than justices of the peace should preside over bail hearings involving violent sexual assaults.

Most of the jury's proposals involved improving the training, organization and day-to-day operations of the justice system. There were very few suggestions for new laws. It was clear from this that the jury generally accepted that existing laws would work if they were applied properly. One of the few changes in the law that was suggested was an amendment to the Criminal Code of Canada that would allow a justice presiding over a bail hearing to remand an accused person in custody for psychiatric assessment to determine if he or she is a danger to the public.

Again, this would seem to be an eminently sensible proposal, but the inquest had heard that this issue is fraught with legal difficulties. There is a danger that the rights of an accused person, who is innocent until proven guilty, could be infringed by being forced to undergo a psychiatric assessment before considering the individual's right to bail. In this — as in other areas where there seemed to be a conflict between individual rights and public safety — the jury asserted that protection of the public should be the paramount consideration.

One of the most frustrating aspects of the evidence that emerged at the inquest was the fact that psychiatrists knew how dangerous Jonathan was and had information about his past violent behaviour, but were not allowed to tell the police or the courts. When Jonathan was assessed at the Clarke Institute after he was released on bail, it was not the court or the Crown, but the defence lawyer who ordered the assessment. A psychiatrist testified that he told the defence lawyer, James Child, that Jonathan was a timebomb. This information was not passed on to the Crown or the police, because it belonged to the defence.

As a result of this case, the Clarke Institute decided not to do any more assessments on behalf of defence lawyers. The coroner's jury recommended that the body which regulates lawyers in Ontario, the Law Society of Upper Canada, change its rules of professional conduct to make defence lawyers obliged to inform the Crown if the accused is talking of harming himself or others.

Medical staff at the jail knew that Jonathan was a suicide risk, but believed that rules of confidentiality prevented them from communicating this to the Crown. The jury recommended that correctional staff be authorized to pass on assessments of a prisoner's suicide risk.

The jury accepted testimony from psychiatrists that confidentiality between doctor and patient is an important principle. Jurors also recognized that psychiatrists and other mental health professionals may be unable to commit patients on an involuntary basis, even when they appear to pose a danger to the public or themselves. These are complex issues to which mental health professionals, legislators and the public obviously need to give more thought.

From a public health perspective, it is important that patients feel they can trust their doctors with details of their emotional problems or embarrassing ailments — otherwise dangerous diseases or conditions may go untreated. Yet, surely there has to be a way for doctors to communicate information to appropriate authorities about patients who pose an imminent threat to public safety? The jury was not able to come up with a suggestion for solving this dilemma.

Since evidence had shown that many police officers did not seem to understand these matters, the jury recommended that regular meetings be held on a community level between police and mental health professionals. These meetings would discuss matters such as which hospitals have secure facilities capable of detaining patients, what information police should provide to psychiatrists when bringing someone in for assessment and whether police can be informed when the patients are released.

Evidence at the inquest had suggested that there are ways of exchanging information without breaching rules of confidentiality. For example, hospitals may not be able to tell police that a dangerous patient has been discharged. But police could phone to ask if the patient still resides in the institution. Crown officers may subpoena confidential medical records for use in court, providing they know what to look for and where to find it. Some witnesses even hinted at the possibility that they might be prepared to provide informal tips to the Crown or police, once they had established a relationship of trust.

Psychiatrists and their lawyers succeeded in persuading the jury that there was no need to change the mental health legislation in a way that would compromise doctors in their role as healers and in their first commitment to their patients. However the jury did recommend that mental health professionals and institutions take vigorous steps to encourage potentially dangerous patients to accept treatment. Psychiatrists were urged to document their findings with respect to the risks posed by such patients and display this information prominently in discharge reports, which would be passed on to family doctors or anybody else treating the patient in future.

Ultimately, psychiatrists were helpless when confronted with Jonathan's problems, because they understood very little about the personality disorders from which he suffered and there were very few treatment opportunities available. The psychiatrists were inclined to simply write him off, suggesting that he could only be dealt with in the criminal justice system.

Sheila Yeo's lawyer, Ray Harris, urged the jury to take a more far-sighted view of this issue. Surely, he argued, it does not make sense to ignore these people's problems until they have harmed or killed innocent people. Harris suggested that society needs to learn more about these personality disorders in order to identify them and provide treatment before it is too late. The jury agreed with his submissions and recommended that funding be provided for research, because "the lack of medical facilities to treat such disorders is detrimental to the safety of our society."

Most of the jury's recommendations were practical and inexpensive to implement. They recognized that resources were limited and proposed reallocating funds in order to give priority to potentially dangerous situations.

Government agencies and other bodies indicated a willingness to move quickly in response to such suggestions. But it remains to be seen what will happen to the more far-reaching proposals, the ones that will inevitably be referred to ministry staff for further study and quite likely never heard of again. The jurors were aware that the recommendations of coroners' juries are very often ignored. They shared Priscilla's concern that the huge exercise in self-examination that the justice system had undertaken through this inquest not be in vain. They therefore proposed amendments to the Ontario Coroners Act which would give coroners more power, compelling the individuals or agencies to whom recommendations are directed to respond in a timely fashion. As the jury was warned before it began its deliberations, changes in the law involve a slow and convoluted process. One year after the inquest, the chief coroner, Dr. Young, said that changes to the Coroner's Act were being considered, but no legislative proposals had been tabled.

In fact, the police and the provincial government ministry responsible for Crown attorneys did move quickly to implement many of the jury's recommendations and anticipated some by putting new measures in place even before the inquest was over. The Hamilton-Wentworth Regional Police set up a specialized sexual assault unit and a new training program which emphasized sensitivity to victims and procedures for arrest, searches and bail release. The idea of checklists was adopted by the police force, which also announced that it would implement new procedures for processing dangerous offenders more carefully in future.

The local Crown attorney's office made immediate changes to ensure that bail was opposed more vigorously in cases involving violence and that prosecutors were better prepared. Better liaison with police was also promised. The attorney-general's ministry announced that it would instruct Crown attorneys to seek a firearms prohibition in any case where a person is released on bail for an offence involving a weapon. Plans were also announced to ensure that victims of violent crime would be invited to bail hearings and given an opportunity to talk to a prosecutor beforehand.

The inquest revealed disturbing weaknesses in the links that should bind all the imperfect components of the justice system into a functioning whole. Lines of communication, procedures and organizational structures were often found to be inadequate and sometimes seemed to be missing altogether.

The inquest provided the potential impetus for creating a more responsive and accountable system. It did so not only by opening the system to outside scrutiny, but also by giving it the benefit of others' expertise. It provided a forum in which police, lawyers, psychiatrists and victims of crime could explain their perspectives and their needs to one another. The jury, representing the community at large, consisted of a nurse, a teacher, a social worker and two business people. They were able to draw on their professional knowledge and experience, as well as the combined expertise of all the witnesses and lawyers at the hearing. Their recommendations were the product of an exchange of information and the evolution of a shared set of insights into the problems. The community now had a vital interest in making sure that the jury's advice would be heeded and its recommendations implemented.

thirteen

CAVEAT

▼

NINA DE VILLIERS' MURDER raised profoundly disturbing issues of the utmost importance to millions of Canadians. Parents could not feel that their daughters were well protected in the light of the problems and attitudes that had allowed Jonathan Yeo to remain at large. Many young women could echo Nina's words concerning the Montreal massacre and say, "It could have been me who was killed."

Many people were not only concerned about the issues and appalled by the story of Nina's murder, but also moved by Priscilla's personal statements about the need to combat violent crime. A grieving mother — who could speak rationally and without rancour, but could never conceal her pain — Priscilla provided a powerful reminder of the human tragedy that violent crime entails.

A nationwide campaign against violence emerged from the public concern and sympathy that Nina's murder evoked. It gathered momentum after the inquest aired all the circumstances and engendered wider publicity for the case. But the campaign had begun several months before the inquest, during the weeks immediately following the discovery of Nina's body in August 1991.

The de Villiers would probably never have initiated a public campaign to change the justice system had they not been frustrated in their efforts to discover the circumstances that led to Nina's death. By the end of September 1991, the media had exposed some of the information about Jonathan Yeo's background that would later be explored in more detail at the inquest. But most people in authority appeared unwilling to respond to any of the questions or criticisms being raised. Some officials issued statements containing incomplete or misleading information. There was no sign of anyone calling for a public inquiry. Appalled that no one in an official capacity was even acknowledging that there was a problem, Rocco de Villiers told a newspaper reporter a month after his daughter's murder, "It seems to be business as usual and too bad about little Nina."

As a surgeon, Rocco routinely conducted investigations when patients died. It was his assumption that one could always learn from things that did not go as expected. He and Priscilla could not understand how three people could have died in bizarre circumstances, raising a host of unanswered questions, and yet there were no plans for any meaningful investigation. He explained in a newspaper interview that he felt compelled to make a public statement: "I really don't want my daughter's death to be completely in vain. If some other poor little girl were to be butchered tomorrow, how could I live with myself if I didn't say anything?"

Priscilla expressed similar views on a radio phone-in show about violent crime. A young policeman phoned in and said he could not do his job anymore because his hands were tied by legislation. Priscilla spontaneously responded by saying that she was going to start a petition to change the laws. She had no idea at the time what such a petition might involve or how to go about starting it. But, as soon as she got home, she began receiving calls from people offering enthusiastic support and practical help.

One of these calls was from Dorothy Leonard, a friend from the tennis club who had offered her moral support at the time of Nina's disappearance. Dorothy was particularly concerned about violent crime and later explained that the idea of starting a petition struck a chord with her because "I thought it was something people could grab on to, something we little people could do."

Priscilla was still unsure about how to proceed and perhaps might have faltered had she not also received a call from Beth Phinney, the Liberal Member of Parliament for the Hamilton Mountain, offering practical advice about how to prepare and present a petition to the federal government. The petition suddenly seemed like a viable proposition.

The de Villiers decided to address the petition to the federal government, partly because they were not getting any response from provincial officials. Ontario government representatives were at that time placing the blame for Jonathan's release on the provisions of the criminal code, which is a federal law. Priscilla and Rocco believed that the only way to get their concerns treated seriously was by exerting pressure on federally elected representatives, the people who pass the laws. The inquest would later show that many of the problems resulted from municipal police forces and provincially appointed Crown prosecutors failing to make full use of the laws available. Nevertheless, it was the federal government's responsibility to legislate measures to protect the public from violent crime and the petition was a way of telling the legislators that much more needed to be done.

Rocco sat down at his computer that weekend and drew up a series of simple clauses which seemed to incorporate all the issues and questions that had been raised in the light of Nina's death. These would later be reviewed by a lawyer and couched in the formal language of a parliamentary petition.

The petition called upon parliament to recognize that crimes of violence against the person are serious and abhorrent to society and to make amendments to the Criminal Code of Canada, together with the laws governing bail and parole. In its preamble the petition stated that Nina's death exposed serious deficiencies in the justice system, which fails to protect many vulnerable people in society, particularly women, children and the disabled.

The first specific clauses drew attention to the law that allows justices of the peace to conduct bail hearings. It seemed obvious to the de Villiers that bail hearings on serious criminal charges involving allegations of violence should be handled by a judge with knowledge and experience in the law.

Accountability in the justice system was another key issue for the de Villiers. They expressed concern in the petition that agents of the Crown cannot be held accountable to the public for actions or omissions in permitting known offenders and accused with violent backgrounds to be free. The law does not let individuals sue the Crown itself for any alleged mistakes or oversights in their work. But the Attorney General and the Crown attorneys can be sued for malicious prosecution. Citizens would have a tough time holding them to account for bail decisions or decisions not to prosecute. As a surgeon, Rocco lived with the constant risk that he could be sued by a patient or family of a patient for alleged malpractice. He felt that Crown lawyers should be in no different position when they made decisions which could result in lives being lost.

The petition also asserted that sentences imposed for crimes of violence did not appropriately reflect society's abhorrence of violence or act as a true deterrent. It suggested that courts or parole boards appear to put the rights of individual criminals over the risk to society in making decisions on early release.

Not all these issues arose directly from the circumstances of Nina's death, but they were all raised by the people who contacted the de Villiers and offered their support. Priscilla saw the petition as a means by which these people could express their concerns to the government. Many Canadians were worried about violent crime in their communities and frustrated because it did not seem that authorities were taking the problem seriously enough.

The first people to get involved with the petition were those who felt their own lives were most closely touched by Nina's murder. Many were members of the racquet club where Nina was killed. Most could remember times when they stood alone after dark in the parking lot where Nina probably first saw her killer. Many of them had children who had played with Nina and gone jogging along the same route. They felt an empathy for the de Villiers which was touched a little with the kind of guilt felt by survivors of a war. They knew that they might just as easily have been victims of this random act of violence. The violence that they had seen on television or heard about in the community had now struck too close to home for them to ignore.

They were a disparate group of people who were initially brought together only by the fact that they played tennis, but now were linked by their common concern about what had happened to Nina. Each of the tennis club members who worked on the petition had her own network of contacts in the community, and amongst them they soon gathered a large pool of volunteers.

The volunteers, who took the petition to shopping malls and circulated it at various community events, were encouraged to find that people were eager to sign and often formed long line-ups waiting to do so. Many who signed the petition, like those who helped organize the campaign, had previously felt helpless in the face of violent crime, perceiving it as an overwhelming global problem with no clear solutions. The petition presented people with a personal appeal from the family of one victim with whom everyone could identify emotionally. It made it clear to all that this was a crime that could and should have been prevented, and it presented specific problems and simple proposals for change.

Priscilla began to give talks to service clubs, church groups and women's organizations about the petition and the issues surrounding Nina's death. She was amazed at the intensity of the anger and distress over violent crime that people communicated. People were afraid of violent crime in their communities, but were evidently frustrated because the justice system seemed insensitive to their concerns and politicians seemed not to be listening. The meetings at which Priscilla spoke invariably drew victims or friends and relatives of victims, who were often anxious to discuss how they were re-victimized by the legal system. Many others were desperate for information about the workings of the justice and penal systems, since sensational media coverage had played upon their fears but seldom provided them with any insight into the issues.

In order to be able to provide people with the information and perspective that they so earnestly craved, Priscilla and others working on the petition began learning more about the justice system and the law. Many in the group felt empowered as they began to understand documents as daunting as the criminal code.

The campaign soon extended beyond the local community. Priscilla was invited as a guest on a nationally televised day-time talk show and this appearance generated further interest from national media. Women's groups and service clubs faxed copies of the petition to other chapters in different parts of the country. Some sympathetic members of parliament circulated the petition in their constituencies. Copies were sent to police associations, churches and women's shelters. Many of those who received copies would fax them on to other groups. In this way the petition was spread far and wide, as Priscilla put it, "like a huge chain letter."

A leaflet accompanying the copies that were sent across the country displayed photographs of Nina and two other murder victims: Brenda Fitzgerald, 23, of Calgary, Alberta, killed in May 1983 by a prisoner who had been released on parole, and Laura Davis, 16, of Moncton, New Brunswick, murdered by a man who had been released on mandatory supervision, a form of parole that is automatically granted after a prisoner has served two-thirds of a sentence. Another photograph, added to later versions of this leaflet, was that of Sian Simmonds, a 19-year-old woman from Langley, British Columbia, killed by a man who had previously been released on bail.

Jean Marquis, the mother-in-law of Jonathan Yeo's other murder victim, was one of the people who responded energetically to the petition campaign. A resident of northern Ontario, she travelled by train through her region, stopping at every station in order to circulate the petition. Not only did other victims and relatives of victims of violent crime come forward to assist in the campaign, but so did people who had never had any involvement with crime and had never participated in any other public campaign in their lives. One such volunteer, a 67-year-old woman, collected 25,000 signatures from various Ontario communities. Another was an octogenarian who gathered several thousand signatures in Belleville, Ontario.

The original plan was to present the petition on December 6, 1991, the second anniversary of the Montreal massacre. But more than 100,000 names had been collected and it seemed that the campaign was still gathering momentum. The de Villiers and their friends decided to let it circulate for a little longer.

In the meantime, Priscilla was asked to join the mother of one of the Montreal massacre victims in making a presentation on gun control laws before the Canadian senate. She spent days talking to police firearms experts, studying the law and scientific journals, before presenting her arguments that somebody accused of a violent act should not be permitted to have a gun or a Firearms Acquisition Certificate. She also proposed the complete registration of all weapons. Her case was a cogent one, since it is probable that Nina would not have been killed if Jonathan had not had a gun. Instead of relying on emotional and personal arguments, however, she also provided senators with a reasoned and well-informed position. The law that was subsequently approved by the Senate included provisions to prohibit people accused of violent crimes from possessing weapons, yet it failed to address Priscilla's concern about gun registration. But Priscilla was invited back to Ottawa to make presentations on other justice issues. Politicians recognized that she and her group had to be taken seriously. They had their own constituency.

The group, which had begun with four women discussing the petition strategy around a coffee table, was beginning to outgrow its informal structure. For Priscilla, it no longer seemed like a personal crusade. While Nina's death had been the stimulus for her involvement, she felt that she was now dealing with broader issues that affected all Canadians. The petition had led her and her friends into a wide range of related activities. Priscilla had scores of invitations to speak at schools and community groups. She was constantly asked to give interviews to the media or participate in lobbying activities on behalf of justice-related issues. There was an obvious need to organize more public meetings at which people could express their views and learn about the system. Priscilla and the petition volunteers were also finding it increasingly difficult to cope with all the calls and letters from victims seeking help or advice and from others wanting to make a contribution to the cause.

A retired corporate executive, the husband of one of the group's founding members, helped set up a non-profit corporation. The group obtained the help of an advertising agency run by one of the tennis club members. The agency helped choose a name and logo for the organization. The acronym CAVEAT was chosen because it has the ordinary meaning of "a warning" and is also used in law to mean "a petition to be heard."

The full name was chosen after the acronym was selected. "Canadians against violence advocating its termination everywhere" seemed a sufficiently general title to encompass flexible and wide-ranging goals. It was important to the members of the group that the word "advocating" was included, since they were anxious not to be perceived as confrontational.

Ann Walsh, whose husband had helped establish the group's corporate structure, explained. "From the very beginning, we had a clear sense of what we wanted. We were very strong about wanting to make sure that our message was clear, that it was constructive and that we didn't want to be seen as yet another group bashing and smashing our way into the system. We don't believe for one minute that everything is wrong, that everything needs to be torn down. And we don't believe that people in the system want to do a bad job."

The goals that were formulated were ambitious. CAVEAT members were seeking to reform the justice system to make it more protective of victims and potential victims. They wanted the system to become more open and accountable to victims and to the public in general. But they also saw their mandate as one of providing a forum for public input on the issue of violent crime. Prevention of violence is preferable to trying to deal with it after it occurs. To this end, CAVEAT proposed to promote a massive public education campaign designed to make violence unacceptable in society. Their model for this was the successful campaign that had been waged during the previous decade to make drunk driving unacceptable to the public and to the courts. The logo selected was a design based on a row of linked human figures with maple leaf patterns in the spaces between them.

CAVEAT was becoming a complex organization with an ever-widening sphere of contacts and access to sophisticated professional help. But, ultimately, what the members of CAVEAT prized most was their own ordinariness. It was important for these people to become involved in the campaign, not because they had an ideological axe to grind or a political agenda, but because they were friends who were shocked by what had happened to Nina. Many were parents who recognized that it could have their been child who died. Others were citizens worried about what had become of their quiet suburban community. They believed it was time for ordinary citizens to take responsibility for what was happening around them.

▼

The level of public interest generated by the petition probably influenced the decision to conduct a full inquest into all the circumstances surrounding Jonathan's death. As we have seen, the inquest was held in the summer of 1992, a few months after CAVEAT was formed.

CAVEAT members attended the hearings and studied the jury's recommendations carefully. Priscilla and other members of the group were determined to ensure that lessons would be learned from the inquest and that its recommendations would be taken seriously. Priscilla's lawyer, Mark Sandler, told the inquest jury, "I'm pledging to you on Mrs. de Villiers' behalf that she won't let your recommendations sit on the shelf."

After the end of the inquest in August 1992, CAVEAT and the petition campaign gained momentum. The inquest had convinced many more people of the need for better crime prevention measures and legislative change.

Individuals from many different backgrounds with a wide range of skills were inspired to get involved. A magazine writer who had been assigned to cover the inquest volunteered to edit the CAVEAT newsletter because she was inspired by Priscilla's courage and her grasp of the issues. The director of an advertising agency saw Priscilla on a breakfast television show and donated the services of his organization to create a hard-hitting promotional campaign. A national magazine and other publications donated space for publication of CAVEAT's public service advertisements.

Community groups, artists, musicians and professional sports stars helped stage fund-raising events. These were valuable, both because of the money that was raised and because they helped CAVEAT make its message known to different audiences. The fact that male sports stars were taking a stand against violence in society was important for CAVEAT members, who felt that their concerns should not be regarded as primarily "a women's issue," but a vital concern for the community at large.

Businesses and clubs donated services, equipment and expertise. With the help of such gifts, CAVEAT was able to set up sophisticated mailing and communications systems. The CAVEAT members, most of whom started off knowing little about political and business systems, worked hard to acquire new skills as they found themselves running a rapidly growing and increasingly complex organization. In so doing, they demonstrated an energy and focus that seemed sadly lacking among the police officers, prosecutors, border guards and other professionals who dealt with Jonathan Yeo.

By spring of 1993, the petition had been signed by more than 1.4 million people. It was to have been presented to the federal government, but Brian Mulroney's surprise resignation prompted a delay. Instead, the group decided to continue to circulate the petition with the goal of obtaining a total of two million signatures and presenting it after the federal election.

CAVEAT's aggressive, but moderate and broadly based campaign undoubtedly played a role in putting concerns about violent crime and crime prevention near the top of the federal political agenda. (Priscilla later became a member of a federally appointed committee which considered proposals for a new law to deal with sexual predators.) CAVEAT campaigned for programs to prevent violent crime, as well as measures for bringing criminals under control. Priscilla was constantly in demand as a speaker at meetings and conferences. Her advice was also sought by government bodies considering new programs and laws.

Meanwhile, CAVEAT continued to promote crime prevention at the community level and particularly in schools. Since most of the members of CAVEAT were homemakers, mothers, teachers, social workers or health professionals, they had a strong belief in the need to tackle the roots of violence in childhood behaviour and social problems. CAVEAT members pooled resources with community agencies, people in the education system and other organizations in developing school programs to combat violence and aggressive sexual stereotypes. Community forums and public education programs were organized.

CAVEAT forged links with other groups in different parts of the country, sharing knowledge, contacts and expertise. It also made its resources available to help the establishment of new groups and to inspire more people to get involved. Organizational handbooks were written and published in order to provide other groups with blueprints for staging education forums.

The petition, the educational tools and the handbooks were all instruments for helping people to focus and direct their energies and concerns. CAVEAT has provided people with ways of overcoming the sense of powerlessness that many feel in the face of violent crime.

Like other members of CAVEAT, Priscilla once lived a relatively insulated life, busy with her family and her work, feeling secure in the belief that she was part of a safe community. She too would turn the page when she read a newspaper story about violent crime, satisfied that this would be dealt with by the authorities entrusted with protecting the public.

Because of her daughter's tragic death, Priscilla was forced to realize that it is no longer possible to have that confidence. She said in an interview, "CAVEAT is saying that crime is our problem. We are taking responsibility. If another child disappears, we are accountable. I feel most Canadians should be accountable. I feel that if you allow innocent people to be hurt and victimized, it's your shame, because you're allowing it to happen."

In her native South Africa, Priscilla had seen problems of violence, hunger and poverty that she felt were beyond her control. In comparison, the task of tackling violent crime in Canada did not seem insurmountable. The inquest exposed specific faults in the justice system which could easily be remedied, given the political will and the resources to do so. The more deep-seated problems of violence in society can obviously not be eradicated overnight, but change still appears possible.

The lessons learned from the murder of one young woman have led to a widespread recognition that everyone needs to get involved in maintaining public safety. The causes of violent crime and its consequences reach deeply into every aspect of community life. Public officials and professionals should not be left to handle the problems alone. The community can no longer blindly trust the criminal justice system to provide protection.

A large number of ordinary Canadians reacted to Nina's death with fear and anger, but they also contributed to CAVEAT with energy, creativity and generosity. Trying to reassert the values of a peaceful, caring society, they are seeking reasonable and practical measures to protect their communities. This has given firm ground for hope.

epilogue

"THE HEALING CIRCLE"

▼

T HE CORONER'S INQUEST ended almost exactly a year after
Nina was killed. A few weeks later, her family commemorated
what would have been Nina's twenty-first birthday, her coming of
age.

During the months before Nina's death, Priscilla had been feeling that her daughter would soon be ready to leave home. Like any
mother, Priscilla had been feeling anxious about seeing the child
whom she had loved and nurtured for 20 years venture out into the
world.

Now it seemed to Priscilla that campaigning to change the justice system was the only thing that she could do for Nina. It was
too late to do anything to make the world safer for her daughter,
but she could do it for other people's children in Nina's name.

Nina had been a gifted and privileged child. Some cynics
observed that Priscilla's campaign was successful precisely because
Priscilla had the money and influence with which to pursue it.
Such critics asked, "Should we not care as much about all the other
murder victims whose stories the public soon forgets? What about
poor and homeless kids who are murdered or abducted? Are their
lives not just as valuable?"

Frustrated by such criticisms, Priscilla retorted, "Don't they
realize that we are speaking for the homeless? We are saying, 'Let's

care about somebody who is randomly, calculatingly, coldly killed, no matter who she is.' And the fact that I've got the means to say it doesn't mean that I shouldn't say it. Nina was privileged. We could give her the background and the nurturing and the space that she needed to develop into a caring and kind human being, someone who could have made a big contribution to the country. It's not to say that she's unique."

One clear lesson to be drawn from Nina's death was that no one — particularly no woman — can be safe as long as society produces and then neglects men like Jonathan, fails to address their problems and allows them to remain at large. The key to Nina's safety lay outside the protective home and affluent community in which she grew up. Other potential victims, no matter who they are and where they live, can only be protected if people work together to heal a social ill that threatens everyone.

When women are killed or assaulted on the streets, there are too many people who question whether the victim was imprudent or provocative. The assumption behind this question is that certain areas at certain times are only safe for men. As violent crime proliferates, increasing numbers of places are being identified as unsafe for women: parking garages, elevators, shopping malls at night, buses and trains at off-peak hours, suburban streets at dusk, parks and hiking trails even in daylight hours. Women who take every reasonable precaution are still vulnerable to attack — like Kristen French, who was abducted in broad daylight on her way home from school, Lynda Shaw, who was lured or dragged from her car at the side of one of Canada's busiest highways, or the victims of the Montreal massacre who were sitting in a university classroom.

Marc Lepine's attack on female engineering students in Montreal was a rearguard attack on the rights and freedoms that women won long ago. Every violent attack on a woman in a public place has a similar impact. If women do not feel safe in the parking lot or elevator of their office building, they do not have true equality in the workplace. The freedom that women supposedly enjoy in our society is illusory, as many still feel they are risking their lives by going out to social gatherings, running, hiking and enjoying nature. And, when many women fear to go out in public places, those places become more deserted and less safe for those who *do* venture out.

Priscilla felt acutely aware of this when she drove past a jogger one evening several months after Nina died. The jogger was a young woman with blonde curly hair running along a quiet tree-lined suburban street at dusk. She looked like Nina and Priscilla wanted to stop and warn her of the danger to which she was exposing herself. But then it occurred to Priscilla that her responsibility was not to warn women of the risk of participating in community life, but to work to end the cycle of violence which makes the community unsafe.

At the same time, Priscilla sensed that her husband, Rocco, and Etienne longed to return to some semblance of a normal family life. Both of them had coped with Nina's death as best they could by throwing themselves into their work. But each of them had found it difficult to reach the point where they were able to do that. Rocco's work as a neurosurgeon involved awesome responsibilities and intense concentration, as well as requiring him to deal frequently with the highly charged emotions of patients and their relatives in life and death situations.

Etienne had been forced to repeat his last year in school, because he found it impossible to focus on his work. He explained in a school essay that the continual press coverage of his sister's death made it impossible to concentrate: "It was only with the conclusion of the inquest in August 1992 that the continuous recountings faded to the occasional mention in a current story. For a full year, my family's grief was front-page news."

It did not seem possible for Priscilla to return to the work to which she had devoted her time and energies before Nina's death. Whenever she tried to work at her landscape painting, she was thrown into a panic by the realization that she could no longer see colour in the same way that she did before. Everything looked grey to her and she believed that she had lost her artistic vision.

Before Nina's death, Priscilla and Sarah Link, a close friend and fellow artist, had agreed that they would put on an exhibition together in a small gallery in Dundas, Ontario. it was scheduled for November 1992 and, as the time grew closer, Priscilla told her friend that she could not paint and did not want to do the show. But Sarah was convinced that it would be therapeutic for Priscilla to do some creative work again. She persuaded Priscilla to collaborate on an installation devoted to spiritual and artistic healing. Two other artists became involved in the project, as well as Pauline Shirt, a traditional healer, descended from the Plains Cree and Saulteaux nations.

They decided to call the show "The Healing Circle," a reference to the ceremonies of aboriginal peoples and to a symbol that many had come to associate with Nina. The cycles of nature were the foundation of Nina's beliefs about life and death. The circle had always been an important symbol to her.

Joan Van Damme, one of the artists who collaborated in the show, had long been preoccupied with the violence that humanity was inflicting on the earth. She believed that the process of healing had to include the environment as well as individuals and the community. Her main contribution to the show was a tent, which recreated the atmosphere of a native sweat lodge. The floor of the tent was strewn with leaves, twigs, pine needles, aromatic cedar chips and moss-covered rocks. In the centre was a large, shallow cement bowl filled with water. Into the bowl, through a small hole in the roof of the tent, photographer Marie José Crête projected slides of a wilderness camp conducted by Pauline Shirt. People were encouraged to sit inside the tent and contemplate the images of a peaceful natural environment shimmering on the surface of the water.

In another part of the gallery was a circle created by Sarah Link comprised of smooth, white porcelain stones and totemic shapes sculpted in clay, surrounding an area covered with pure white sand. The serenity of this circle contrasted sharply with the disturbing images that Priscilla had placed on the walls around it. On one wall was a piece entitled "Nina's circle," consisting of large charcoal drawings of the faces of six of Nina's friends, all seared with intense sorrow. These portraits were arranged as a diptych, three faces in each frame, with a space between them where Nina should have been where the circle had been broken.

On the opposite wall was Priscilla's circle, a row of grey clay masks of Sarah, Priscilla and five women from CAVEAT. These masks had been baked in an oven fired with pine cones and pine needles which had spat embers onto the clay so as to roughen its surface with random patterns. The scarred faces looked stern and implacable.

These were images of people who had been brought together by Nina's death. Although each of them appeared deeply wounded and isolated in her grief, there was a strong solidarity amongst them. They suggested the power of a community that is determined to bring about change. In order to suggest that their campaign was not about one murdered woman but directed against all forms of violence, Priscilla placed, on an adjacent wall, a lithograph depicting violent images from South Africa. It was entitled, "And the women weep."

Several hundred people crowded into the small gallery on the opening night of the show. Many found that the art show helped them to deal with their own pain. Visitors kept returning to the gallery and seemed to use it as a place for contemplation. Some people wrote poems, which they posted on the walls of the gallery or sent to the de Villiers.

For Priscilla, like others who grieve for victims of violence, it still seems easier to help heal the world than to fill the void that was left at the centre of her own family life. She hopes that some day it might be possible for her to resume her ordinary life, have fun play-ing tennis and create beauty in her art. But that will have to wait until she finishes campaigning to make her community and her country safer for other people's children. Priscilla lives with the understanding that no man, woman or child can be truly free until everyone can walk the streets without fear.

afterword
by Priscilla de Villiers

▼

I CANNOT PAINT BECAUSE I cannot see the colour in the world as I always could. Music has become a source of intense pain. There was a time, not so long ago, that I gloried in music of every conceivable type.

My father has always loved music and my earliest memories were of sitting on his lap, crying over the life and poetry of Frost, Keats and Shelley while Mozart, Beethoven or Bach filled the room and kept the darkness at bay. My musical education was broadened when I married Rocco but it was through Nina that I learned to listen to baroque music and appreciate the compositions of Philip Glass. Etienne has taught me to love jazz, the more authentic the better.

I even used to dance while working for an art exhibition; a large, middle-aged woman, capering alone in my studio, with a palette in one hand and a brush in the other, infused with the joy of creativity, the joy of music, of life.

I do not dance anymore.

I have become an expert in avoidance coping. I avoid obvious situations that will tear the fragile skin that has grown over my grief. I have reached the stage, mainly at night, when I relax my guard and try to sleep — but then I confront the horror and terror of Nina's death, in the dirt, alone.

Unfortunately I am not unique. As I go about the country tilting at the windmills of violence and attitudes to violence, I meet so many people who are also suffering this deep and needless pain. The father who had just sat in court and looked into his daughter's killer's eyes for six minutes, a man out on bail for murder. The mother whose 12-year-old daughter was raped by a stranger and who is told that it is against his rights to be tested for HIV unless he wants to and that she will just have to wait. The mother whose young son was molested by a man who was on probation for other offences against children and who learned that the offender has once again been released on probation. There are so many others. They phone, they write and they come up to me in shopping malls and at speaking engagements.

Their pain is palpable. They are bewildered by a system that could so obviously fail to protect the vulnerable members of society. So am I. We are the victims.

It is a fallacy that there is one victim of crime. There are many levels of hurt caused by callous indifference to the right to life, liberty and security of others. In fact, everyone in our society is being victimized in some way by the brutality of relatively few people. When I go into schools I meet frightened, demoralized young people. Young women do not feel free to make career choices that will involve shiftwork or localities that will leave them vulnerable. Parents are terrified so that they overreact and curtail their children's freedom to a paralyzing degree.

Our young people are the most affected by the rising violence in the schools, in their homes and on the streets. If we break the silence, if we discuss the pressures of our changing world we can raise their awareness and help them gain the insight and the skills that will empower them to deal with many of the problems that confront them.

Stricter laws, stringently enforced, are necessary to give a strong message that violence will not be tolerated in Canada. However, laws alone will not be successful unless they are supported by a change in attitude to violence in entertainment, violence in sport and violence as a solution in daily life.

As CAVEAT gains in stature I am humbled and often afraid that I will not be able to live up to the unqualified support that more and more people are lending to our campaign. I owe so many so much.

I have to start painting again. Art has been integral to my life for as long as I can remember and I have been mourning the loss of my inner eye, of my other self as well. That is a loss that I can and must confront, to find a way to restore that part of myself at least.

Music, however, is another matter. I cannot escape it. As I sit here a line from a song that Nina used to sing runs in my head.

"You smile and the angels sing...."

Priscilla de Villiers
Burlington, June 1993